Drivel!

A Decade of Jargon and Gobbledygook

as recorded by the

Plain English Campaign

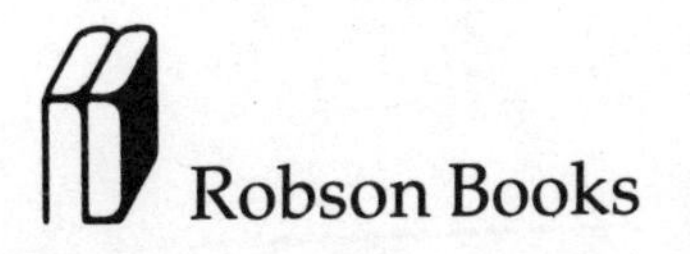

Robson Books

To the hundreds of campaigners who have stood up to say: 'The bull stops here.'

First published in Great Britain in 1994 by Robson Books Ltd,
Bolsover House, 5-6 Clipstone Street, London W1P 7EB

British Library Cataloguing in Publication Data
A catalogue record for this title is available from the British Library

ISBN 0 86051 949 X

Design by Harold King

The Message of Support from HRH The Prince of Wales first appeared in the Plain English Campaign's Awards brochure, 1992 and appears here with his permission.

Typeset by Harrington & Co.
Printed in Great Britain by Butler & Tanner Ltd.
Frome and London

Contents

A Message of Support from HRH The Prince of Wales — v

Introduction — vi

Drivel — 1

Plain English at Work — 89

The Plain English A-Z Guide to Alternative Words — 101

ST. JAMES'S PALACE

Due to a frequent regrettable inability to prevent my presence in other locations, I find that I must convey to you my goodwill in a correspondence format. It was when I was still a juvenile future constitutional figurehead substitute that I first became sensitised by my mother-tongue abuse awareness. How many of us, I wonder, when faced with pretentious gobbledegook and empty jargon, experience a kick start into despair mode? My feelings towards all of you are, attitudinally, those of enormous encouragement . . . . .

God bless the Plain English Campaign.

Charles

INTRODUCTION

As this is a book devoted to encouraging the use of plain English and exposing the worst excesses of jargon and gobbledygook, we'd better begin with a swift explanation of these two horrors.

There's an interesting story here. Although most of what follows is written English, both 'jargon' and 'gobbledygook' originated as descriptions of sounds – the sounds of birds to be strictly accurate.

'Jargon' can boast the longer history. The word fell out of use in the thirteenth century only to be revived in modern times, presumably when the need for it arose. When Geoffrey Chaucer used the word 'jargon' in his 'Merchant's Tale' he was describing a confused twittering and chattering of birds. And when we look at the jargon produced by banks, multi-national companies and so many of today's 'merchants', the confused twittering comes through loud and clear.

'Gobbledygook' has a more specific reference to birds – turkeys! The word was invented by a Texan, the appropriately named Henry Maverick. He likened the gobble-gobble sound made by turkeys to the convoluted, pretentious and frequently meaningless language favoured by bureaucracy. His word became commonplace and so, regrettably, did its subject matter. That's why the Plain English Campaign is delighted to be expanding internationally and taking the fight back across the Atlantic to continue Mr Maverick's crusade in the United States.

When the Plain English Campaign was founded none of us thought that fifteen years later we would still be coming across new forms of gobbledygook. But despite all our efforts, the problem never went away. As fast as we got rid of one form of gobbledygook, another reared its ugly head. And now new dangers, such as Euro-speak and management jargon confront us.

We don't want to 'downgrade' English or limit writers of literature. We just want public information to be written clearly. Without this we have no chance of understanding our rights and responsibilities and no chance to act on the information we receive.

Here we've collected some of the choicest examples of officialese and other gobbledygook that have come our way. They come from a wide range of sources and, to give many of those sources credit, a lot of them have set about mending their ways and simplifying their messages. That's why we've spared their blushes and disguised their identities.

In the Plain English at Work chapter you'll find some examples of how plain English can be used to turn previously unintelligible prose into straightforward language that anyone can understand. And to help you write plain English yourself, there is a guide to alternative words which should set you off on the right path.

If what follows raises a laugh (or a gasp) we hope it will spread the message wider. Research has revealed that sloppy letter-writing alone costs the UK £6 billion a year as a result of mistakes, inefficiency and lost business. As campaign founder, Chrissie Maher, said, 'I think we are here to stay.'

If further evidence is needed, here are some examples of the kind of bull people are still saying (rather than writing). And to be scrupulously fair, we'll begin with Chrissie Maher herself.

The Things People Say

Chrissie Maher, Plain English Campaign:

'It's as black as the ace of diamonds.'

'No use bolting the door after the elephant has got out.'

'A bird in the hand is worth two on the bus.'

'I'm up to my kneeballs in work.'

Menzies Campbell MP, on BBC's *Question Time:*

'It is a myth that women get pregnant in order to have children.'

Ted Dexter, former England cricket boss, trying to explain away another England defeat at the hands of the Australians:

'Maybe we are in the wrong sign. Maybe Venus is in the wrong juxtaposition with something else. I don't know.'

Nigel Short, at the recent world chess championship which he lost to Gary Kasparov:

'I think I had an advantage today because I only noticed I was completely winning just before the end.'

US army spokesman in Somalia, talking on BBC's *World At One*:

'The status quo was not resolving itself in a satisfactory way.'

Ian Loader, criminologist, talking about the police:

'The locus of the state's use of coercive force.'

Helen Haste explains that men are often nasty to women:

'Cultural ways of dealing with the overwhelming forces of sexuality reflect variations in projections in both the causes of sexual chaos and the control of that chaos on to women.'

Dan Quayle, former vice-president of the USA:

'We offer the party as a big tent. How we do that (recognise the big tent philosophy) within the platform, the preamble to the platform or whatnot, that remains to be seen. But the message will have to be articulated with great clarity.'

Duncan Higgins struggles to explain the thinking behind his exhibition of 'black paintings':

'These pieces taken individually or as a whole are part of a particular on-going attempt to embrace a complex set of both personal and cultural/historical questions and ideas. Central to this is bound the question of conception, representation and presentation. To realise and make visible these questions the pieces use and embody a wide range of pictorial methods, texts and materials, in an attempt to contain within the pieces the many layers of reality and experience.'

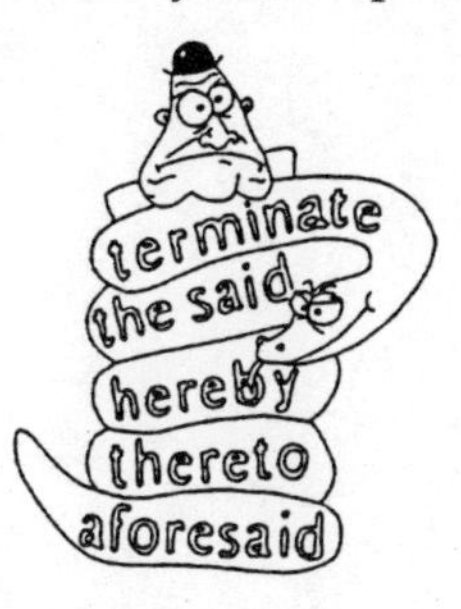

Saddam Hussein makes things clear to his ministers:

'Every one of you should be at your ministry at eight in the morning. Only those who are sick will be authorised to contact the cabinet secretary to inform him of the problem. That will enable us to know that someone is sick, to inquire after his condition and to wish him a speedy recovery.

'But all those who are not sick should be present at 8 am. I don't want any other excuses. Those who pretend to have slept late have no excuse. Instead of going to bed at two in the morning, they should retire at one. If they don't get to bed before two, even though they have to get up at five or six, they will have to learn to go to bed earlier.'

Gavin Partington, GMTV's political correspondent, explains the reason for the latest cabinet reshuffle:

'This will give ministers a chance to grab hold of their briefs before the next election.'

Mike Lubor, the American commentator, tries to explain the rules of soccer:

'A free kick is an opportunity to kick a dead ball while remaining relatively unmolested by the opposition.'

James Sanger, 'multi-instrumentalist', describes his music:

'Ethno-oriental micro-mental tonal trip-faced fantasy tuned adult lullabies for the nineties.'

DRIVEL

Just what is a bed? It's a big question, so the NHS have produced a big answer:

BED

A device or arrangement that may be used to permit a patient to lie down when the need to do so is a consequence of the patient's condition rather than a need for active intervention such as examination, diagnostic investigation, manipulative treatment, obstetric delivery or transport.

Beds, couches, or trolleys are also counted as hospital beds where:

a) used regularly to permit a patient to lie down rather than for merely examination or transport. (e.g. in a day surgery ward.)

b) used whilst attending for a specific short procedure taking an hour or less such as endoscopy, provided that such devices are used only because of the active intervention and not because of the patient's condition.

c) used regularly as a means of support for patients needing a lengthy procedure such as renal dialysis (includes special chairs etc.).

d) used regularly to allow patients to lie down after sedation.

NB: A device specifically and solely for the purpose of delivery should not be counted as a bed.

Available staffed beds: occupied or ready for occupation on the last day of the quarter under review, i.e. in which patients are being or could be treated without any changes in facilities or staff being made.

Includes cots in special care baby units and intensive therapy units for babies.
Excludes:

a) Labour (first and second stage) as distinct from maternity beds.
b) Beds in reception wards, unless in permanent use in psychiatric hospitals.
c) Temporary beds (or stretchers) unless in permanent use in psychiatric hospitals.
   Temporary bed: erected additional to the ward complement and dismantled within 24 hours of being erected. A bed erected for an emergency, but left up on account of pressure for a succession of patients, should be regarded as a temporary bed until dismantled.
d) Observation or recovery beds used for only a few hours, whether in out-patients departments or recovery units;

You probably want to have a lie-down now...

An NHS executive: the early years

When dealing with a bolshie customer, you can get your own back by apologizing sweetly and calling him a liar at the same time. Transparent Windows Ltd of Bullville:

Dear Mr Jones,
Thank you for your letter dated 13/7/82 explaining both your satisfaction as well as your frustration which is fully understandable to appreciate. All comments made by yourself are not entirely true to form regarding information passed but are accepted in total as constructional criticism in the hopes that a repeat situation such as endured by you does not ensue. Would you please however accept our sincere apologies from all within our Company as we do not wish to leave anybody with a sour taste and find enclosed the typed guarantee. Once again profuse apologies for an unacceptable delay which became beyond our control as it stemmed from the extruding suppliers.

The ability to empathize with the reader is an important part of the official writer's art. Sadly, not all manage it. Judging by this letter from a local authority officer, the writer seems to think that empathy is something you buy in packets of twenty:

'In reply to your recent enquiry regarding your entitlement to retirement benefits if you were to be retired under the Voluntary Redundancy Scheme; when the added years awarded to you under the Scheme exceed 6.2/3rd years, there is a reduction of an amount equal to 30% of your redundancy payment in respect of each year (and part year) of service in excess of this. The amount is deducted from your additional lump sum, but if the said amount is greater than the additional lump sum, the outstanding balance is capitalised and deducted from the additional pension. When the added years awarded are 6 years 243 days or less there is no reduction in your compensation.'

Does anyone have a light?

When a management magazine featured an article on 'organizational culture' one extract offered a refreshingly new approach to the subject:

The strength of a culture depends on three things; first, the pervasiveness of the norms and behaviours in the explicit culture, and the pervasiveness of the values and beliefs in the implicit culture – ie the proportion of the members of the social group that firmly hold to the norms and beliefs. Secondly, cultural strength depends on the pervasiveness of the beliefs and behaviours themselves –
ie the range of behaviours and the range of beliefs and values which the culture sets out to control.

It's said that the pen is mightier than the sword. With gobbledygook this is undeniably true. Try to work out what this letter from a bank means and you'll see what we mean:

It was Resolved;
THAT pursuant to the RESIGNATION/DEATH/REMOVAL of the undermentioned;

from the Office(s) specified, 'Piggy' Bank PLC be and is hereby directed that the authority of the above mentioned to bind the Customer pursuant to the existing Mandate by the Customer to 'Piggy' Bank PLC is terminated PROVIDED THAT all authorities, instructions, instruments and transactions authenticated by the above mentioned pursuant to the Customer's said mandate to 'Piggy' Bank PLC and purporting to have been given, made, issued, or entered into prior to receipt by 'Piggy' Bank PLC of notice of this resolution shall have the effect as between the Customer and 'Piggy' Bank PLC as though this resolution had never been passed.

Utter Drivel!

One of the ironies of the computer revolution is that office equipment designed to speed up communication frequently comes wrapped in terms and conditions that are largely meaningless to the people using it. Photocopiers are a good example and here's a photocopier hire agreement to make the point:

This Agreement constitutes the entire agreement between the Customer and Confusion Photocopiers (Obfuscation) Ltd. and

no representation, statement, condition or warranty not contained in this Agreement shall be binding on Confusion Photocopiers (Obfuscation) Ltd. The said terms shall prevail notwithstanding any variance or conflict with the terms and conditions sought to be imposed by the Customer and the Customer's signature hereof and/or acceptance of delivery of the Equipment shall be conclusive thereof.
If the Customer wishes to lease or finance the purchase of the Equipment through a third party, then Confusion Photocopiers (Obfuscation) Ltd. shall allow the Customer to assign the obligations of payment contained in paragraphs 5(a) and 5(b) to an assignee and in the event title to the Equipment shall pass to such assignee from Confusion Photocopiers (Obfuscation) Ltd. after these payments have been made notwithstanding paragraphs 9(c) and 11 of the Maintenance and Service Contract.

This kind of gobbledygook gets right up our noses:

Uses
These nasal drops are indicated for the prophylactic treatment of allergic rhinitis (seasonal and perennial).

Directions for use
Since therapy with the nasal drops is essentially prophylactic, it is important to maintain regular dosage, as distinct from using the drug intermittently to relieve symptoms.
Adults and children: Instil two drops into each nostril six times daily, or as directed by your doctor.

Contra-indications
These nasal drops are contraindicated in patients with known hypersensitivity to any of the constituents of the formulation. The constituents are sodium cromoglycate, sodium edetate, benzalkonium chloride and purified water.

Fluffy Cakes Limited provide a mouth-watering recipe for trifle sponges:

TRIFLE RECIPE
Ingredients
1 Packet Fluffy Trifle Sponges
1 Packet of Jelly
1 Can of Fruit
1 Pint of Custard
1/4 Pint Whipping Cream

Method

Line base of dish with Fluffy Trifle Sponges. Make up jelly using water and juice from canned fruit. Leave to set. Make up using custard and leave to cool. Pour cooled custard over jelly, top with cream and decorate as required.

So economical is the recipe that there's even a can of fruit left at the end.

The writer of this county council letter waxes lyrical on the subject of teaching art:

The Authority does not see the role and functions of art in education simply in terms of the communication of observations of the made and natural world, but sees expressive and symbolic communications of the inner world as having equal and legitimate significance.

The demise of the Inner London Education Authority did not remove the ILEA from London's memory. In fact, readers of a

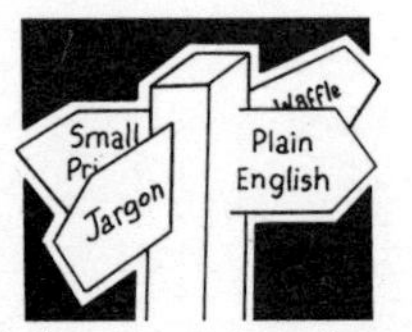

document from one of the London boroughs might be forgiven for believing that the ILEA was still alive and kicking:

The Government have stated that "safety net" arrangements (*i.e. for community charge*) will need to allow for the transfer of education responsibilities to the Boroughs as a result of the abolition of ILEA, although the details of the working of the safety net have not been announced. Given, however, that the Governments intention is that the overall effect of the 'safety net' should be that the Inner London Boroughs in 1990/91 will be able to spend on education at a similar level to their apportionment of ILEA's pattern of spending with community charges on average at the level which would have been needed had ILEA remained in being, there is no reason to suppose that the education safety net will operate any differently from that already proposed."

With rate payers receiving letters like this, the Poll Tax must have been seriously flawed for them not to have welcomed it as a vast improvement:

"Collection rate: the billing authority's estimate, in accordance with 'the 1992 Regulations', of the proportion of, in essence, the amounts payable and the amounts transferable pursuant to directions under section 98 of the 1988 Act (eg from its general to its collection fund in respect of council tax benefit) in respect of its council taxes for a year which it estimates are likely ultimately to be paid and transferred."

Even when insisting they will not be parting with their money, some writers manage to obscure their own safeguards with considerable success:

The Guarantor shall not by paying any sum due hereunder or by any means or on any ground claim or recover by the institution of proceedings or the threat of proceedings or otherwise such sum from the Contractor or claim any set-off or counterclaim against the Contractor or prove in competition with the Employer in respect of any payment by the Guarantor hereunder or be entitled in competition with the Employer to claim or have the benefit of any security which the Employer holds or may hold for any money or liabilities due or incurred by the Contractor to the Employer and in case the Guarantor receives any sums from the Contractor in respect of any payment of the Guarantor hereunder the Guarantor shall hold such monies in trust for the Employer so long as any sums are payable (contingently or otherwise) under this Agreement.

Warnings about the risks of parting with your money can be similarly opaque:

The Purchaser hereby admits and confirms that he has inspected the property and has not been induced to enter into this agreement by or on reliance upon any statement either oral or in writing by the Vendor or by any agent servant or representative of the Vendor or by any third party other than the Vendor's Solicitors written replies to any written enquiries made by the Solicitors acting for the Purchaser prior to the date hereof and accepts that if any such statement has been made other than as aforesaid it was not made as a condition warranty or representation or for the purpose of adducing the Purchaser to enter into this agreement and shall not obviate the need for the Purchaser to make appropriate Searches and enquiries of the relevant Local and public Authorities and utilities and to inspect the property and to commission such surveys and testing of the property in relation to the Purchaser's proposed use of the property and accordingly all conditions warranties or other terms implied by statute or common law are hereby excluded to the fullest extent permitted by law.

Which means, in case you were wondering: 'Don't try to complain about the house. We've said nothing, we know nothing and who are you anyway?'

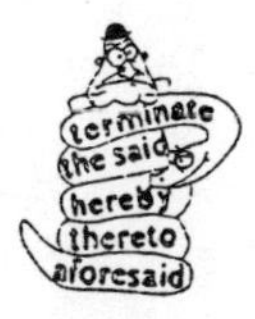

You will get benefit sooner ... or later:

Housing services are currently making changes to the way benefit is paid. The changes mean that we will be able to pay benefit more quickly.
In order to help us to be more responsive to any changes in your circumstances, cheques will be posted out slightly later. From the cheque dated 22 January 1994 we will post your cheque by second class mail on a Friday rather than a Wednesday. This means you will receive your fortnightly benefit cheque slightly later than you do at present.

Historians will record that the Community Charge was not a rip-roaring success. Perhaps it got off to a poor start in Scotland because it was not fully understood:

I am sending you a copy of your new entry, your previous entry as amended or notification of the deletion of your previous entry, as the case may be, together with this notice in terms of section 15(5) of the Abolition of Domestic Rates Etc. (Scotland) Act 1987 ("the Act"), as amended by paragraph 24(4) of Schedule 12 to the Local Government Finance Act 1988 ("the 1988 Act"). In order to show what the amendment is, I am also sending (except in the case of a new entry) a copy of your previous entry.

And this needs rewriting, a rewrite or to be rewritten, as the case may be:

Reduced earnings allowance is payable from 17.9.92 to 26.10.93 (both dates included) at the weekly rate of £35.36. This is because the claimant's probable standard of remuneration in his regular occupation is £315.00 and the probable standard of remuneration in employed earner's employment which is suitable in his case, namely bookkeeper, which he is not incapable of following as the result of the relevant loss of faculty is £104.00

Common sense plays a big part in putting together a clear, concise piece of writing. But, as this football match programme suggests, sense is anything but common:

"We cannot fall into the trap of committing practical haplography. It is also a dangerous feeling to consider that where we are in the League is of acceptable standard because standard is relevant to the standards we have set, which thereby may well indicate that we have not aspired to the standard which we set ourselves."

"We must be the harbingers and nothing less than this can be acceptable."

Something of an own goal, perhaps?

It's good to know that standards aren't falling everywhere:

Dear Sir,
Thank you for your enquiry for our Gracenet cricket nets. The standard width for cricket nets is 9ft (2.44 metres). We therefore have pleasure in setting out below our prices for the standard 8ft width and also at the same time a price for our standard width of 4 metres (13ft).

It can be just as complicated when you try to claim money to which you are entitled. Here is a prime example:

Provided always that should any payment to such person under the Criminal Injuries Compensation Scheme or the said statutory provisions fall below a sum which would otherwise be payable under the Reaper UK Fatal Accident Scheme, but for the exclusion in Paragraph 3c (i) above, then Reaper UK using the discretion conferred upon it by Paragraph 5 below may pay a sum equal to the difference between the Criminal Injuries Compensation Scheme payment and the sum otherwise payable under the Reaper UK Fatal Accident Scheme.

Making your vote in a free and fair election is one of the touchstones of a civilized democratic society, for which generations have struggled. Following in this noble tradition come these voting procedures drawn up by a British centre of higher education. They present a formidable intellectual challenge before you even consider who to vote for:

You should continue to express preferences only as long as you are able to place successive candidates in order.

A later preference is considered only if an earlier preference has a surplus above the quota required for election; or is excluded because of insufficient support.

Under no circumstances can a later preference count against an earlier preference.

Public servants sometimes offer a safe haven to the almost extinct words which occasionally alight on their desks. One such rarity survives in this section of a rates bill, where the plural of the species, equally unusual, is also to be found:

The amount assessed upon you for the above period is as detailed below and payment of the first moiety is hereby requested by one of the methods listed overleaf. You may pay both moieties at the same time, if you so wish.

In case you were wondering, that's 'moiety' in the sense of 'A moiety of lager and a packet of peanuts, please'.

Some job advertisements are written in foreign languages and a knowledge of those languages is a key requirement for the job. In many respects the same may be true of this advertisement from a national newspaper:

Moving from hierarchical structures to a process-based architecture, our success has been based on consistent, integrated teamwork and quality enhancement through people. By ensuring consistency in the development and integration of process plans, you will facilitate the management processes to develop implementation plans for the processes they manage. You will also be involved in business plan modelling, rolling plan methodologies and the measurement of process effectiveness.

As Integration Planner, your position will be at the interface of the personal, planning, implementation and measurement matrix.

We would like the person who got the job to come forward and answer the following: 'What do you do?'

If music be the food of love, then prose be the meat of thought – and this advert by Barber, Bullrush and Bright is that little bit of gristle you spend hours chewing over without getting anywhere:

Barber, Bullrush and Bright is pioneering the development of research-based internal and external communications strategy.

Unlike the generalists of traditional PR consultancy we are focusing on providing clients with a high value-added contribution in:

- facilitating internal acceptance of change through attitudinal programmes
- determining and articulating market positioning
- managing the overall process of communications
- advising on the resourcing and management of corporate and internal communications functions.

Section 16 of the Local Government (Miscellaneous Provisions) Act is a good example of why many people think the time has come to let MPs work the same hours as most other people, instead of struggling on long after the rest of us are tucked up in bed:

(1) Where, with a view to performing a function conferred on a local authority by any enactment, the authority considers that it ought to have information connected with any land, the authority may serve on one or more of the following persons, namely –

a) the occupier of the land; and

b) any person who has an interest in the land either as freeholder, mortgagee or lessee or who indirectly receives rent for the land; and

c) any persons who, in pursuance of an agreement between himself and a person interested in the land, is authorised to manage the land or to arrange for the letting of it,

a notice specifying the land and the function and the enactment which confers the function and requiring the recipient of the notice to furnish to the authority, within a period specified in the notice (which shall not be less than fourteen days beginning with the day on which the notice is served), the nature of his interest in the land and the name and address of each person whom the recipient of the notice believes is the occupier of the land and of each person who he believes is, as respects the land, such person as is mentioned in the provisions of paragraphs (b) and (c) of this subsection.

Often enough the tone of official letters is inoffensive, even polite, to the ratepayer or taxpayer. A more salty style prevails in Bullville Council's housing department:

> After the acceptance of a housing application, the applicant must immediately notify the Director of Health and Housing if he changes his address or if there is any alteration in his family circumstances. Failure to give such notification will render the application void and it will be deleted from the housing waiting list with little or no prospect of it ever being reinstated thereon.

Such an approach can make the meaning a little too clear. Another Council's legal officer wrote to a council tenant who was late paying her rent:

Let me make one thing clear: if for any reason we don't get the money, you'll be out of that house so fast it'll make your head spin and we won't be rehousing you.

Most banks display commendable caution in lending money to would-be house-buyers. Some test the borrower's resolve by devising savings and mortgage conditions like these:

8.15 not to use or permit the Property to be used save for private residential purposes;

8.17 notwithstanding Paragraph 8.15 above, in the event of

the Company expressly authorising the Borrower in writing to carry on a business on the Property, then the Borrower covenants to use his best endeavours to obtain and maintain all licences and renewals of licences necessary or desirable in relation to the carrying on of the said business on the Property and if and when required by the Company to obtain a transfer or transfers of the said licences or any of them to the Company or its nominee and for the purposes of this paragraph the Borrower hereby irrevocably appoints the Company to be the attorney of the Borrower and his nominee to apply for and to obtain from time to time renewals of the licences hereby assigned and to sign all proper notices and other documents and to do all necessary acts for assigning or transferring the said licences to the Company or as the Company may otherwise require and the borrower hereby covenants with the Company to confirm whatever the Company may do or purport to do under the power of attorney herein contained.

One resident of Bullville thought he'd happened upon a bizarre relic of a forgotten language when this document plopped onto his doormat. Unfortunately, further investigation revealed it to be a letter from a nearby housing association. First, a warning:

Please find enclosed our notice proposing a new rent. This is a legal document which we are obliged to issue and may be difficult to understand.

And then:

Landlord's Notice Proposing a New Rent Under An Assured Periodic tenancy

1. This is to give notice that as from 05 July 1993 your landlord proposes to charge a new rent.

   The new rent must take effect at the beginning of a new period of the tenancy and not earlier than any of the following:-

a) the minimum period after this notice was served, (the minimum period is:-
   - in the case of a yearly tenancy, six months,
   - in the case of a tenancy where the period is less than a month, one month, and,
   - in any other case, a period equal to the period of the tenancy.)

b) the first anniversary of the start of the first period of the tenancy except in the case of:-
   - a statutory periodic tenancy, which arises when a fixed term assured tenancy ends, or
   - an assured tenancy which arose on the death of a tenant under a regulated tenancy,

c) if the rent under the tenancy has previously been increased by a notice under section 13 or a determination under section 14 of the Housing Act 1988, the first anniversary of the date on which the increased rent took effect.

Brief but impenetrable – is this about land or underwear?

Every person who, if a general vesting declaration were made in respect of all the land comprised in the order in respect of which notice to treat has not been given, would be entitled to claim compensation in respect of any such land is invited to give information to the authority making the declaration in the prescribed form with respect to his name and address and the land in question.

When is insurance necessary and when is it not? Here's a reasonable explanation:

If premises were not a reasonable foreseeable cause of danger to anyone acting in a way in which a human being could be reasonably expected to act in circumstances which might reasonably be expected to occur in light of the purpose for which the premises were made available, it would not be reasonable to require an individual to take further measures against unknown and unexpected events towards their safety.

On a 'dollars for drivel' basis, this is a great deal. It's good to know that certain underwriters can overwrite too ...

THIS IS TO CERTIFY that in accordance with the authorisation granted under Contract Number 010 by Underwriters at Jones's whose names and the proportions underwritten by them, which will be supplied on application, can be ascertained by reference to the said Contract which bears the Seal of Jones's Policy Signing Office, and where it is agreed that should the Insured participate on any insuring Syndicate hereunder Underwriters' percentage lines shall be increased proportionately to replace the common Syndicate(s) line under this Contract and that the common Syndicate(s) interest in respect of that of that insured be excluded, and in consideration of the premium paid, as specified herein, the said Underwriters are hereby bound, each for his own part and not for another, their Heirs, Executors and Administrators, to insure in accordance with the terms and conditions attached hereto.

A report into the possible leasing of residential homes begins with this deathless sentence:

"In pursuance of Minute No. 104/1993, the Committee considered a joint report by the Chief Executive, Director, County Treasurer and County Valuer and Estates Officer upon the consideration by the Ad Hoc Sub-Committee on the Establishment of Trusts and other 'Arms Length' Organisations of the strategic options and operational and financial implications of the future management and contracting arrangements for residential care which had included an appraisal of the financial pressures on the Social Services Committee's capital programme in respect of the requirement to bring transferred and retained Homes up to registration standards."

What a minute that must have been.

Salary reviews need delicate handling when they are presented to staff. One staff association adopted the cunning solution of laying out a few ground rules that no one (not even the author) could understand:

Underpinning the resolve and determination of the Association to move forward, the result of new positive thinking, was a simple, but totally honest assessment of the capabilities of the Association, the ability of its very small professional staff and the harnessing of all known resources by them, as a back up service, not forgetting additional finance in terms of expenditure for special survey projects and printing costs and even the necessity of additional part-time staff, allied to the firm, inescapable conclusion, that all future applications to the Corporation would have to be presented in such a way, so as to be supported by facts, proven statistics and overwhelming evidence of argument in favour, wholly, totally and absolutely outweighing any negative rejection and making it possible for an acceptable compromise to be mutually agreed, without the trappings of political influences or intervention.

Great detective fiction didn't die with Agatha Christie. This Council can still make a good mystery out of a public notice:

BULLVILLE LEISURE CENTRE JOINT COMMITTEE

After 30th May, 1981 there will at times be restrictions on the total number of persons permitted at any one time in the Bullville Leisure Centre, Bullville.

The restrictions will not apply after 6.00 pm on any Monday, Tuesday, Wednesday, Thursday or Friday or after 11.30 am on any Saturday or Sunday or at all on Glasgow Fair Monday.

At all other times the restrictions may apply but it is expected that there will be many exceptions – i.e. days on which the restrictions will not apply at all and other days on which the restrictions will not apply after a time earlier than 6.00 pm or 11.30 am as the case may be.

Unfortunately the exceptions are not predictable and whether or not there will be an exception on any particular day will not normally be known before 4.30 pm on the preceding day.

Persons seeking up-to-date information as to what restrictions will apply on any particular day should telephone Bullville 12121 either on the day in question or after 4.30 pm on the preceding day.

For the sake of clarity, some officials assume that their readers have no knowledge of the subject about which they're writing. Just occasionally this can be taken too far, as this fire-safety letter shows:

Fire is a basic chemical reaction in which multiple components interact to create the burning event. Resultant products of this fire reaction include the familiar flames, heat and smoke which are easily detected by the human senses of sight, touch and smell.

People often ask the Plain English Campaign to write an effective friendly, easily read hire document. We tell them they couldn't do better than look through the following contract from a car-hire company, study its style, its wording, its layout, its structure, tone and grammar. Then write something as different from it as possible:

In the event of breakdown the Owner will at his own expense collect the vehicle and effect repairs thereto provided always that if the repairs aforesaid are rendered necessary by reason of any neglect, default of breach of this Agreement or abuse of misuse of the vehicle by the Renter or Driver, the Renter will pay to the Owner on demand the cost of such collection and the cost of repairs. The cost of any repairs carried out on the instructions of the Renter or Driver without the prior written approval of the Owner shall be the responsibility of the Renter.

Warnings of price increases can be phrased in many ways, from the awfully frank to the frankly awful. This one becomes completely tangled by the end of the paragraph:

In the event of increases in the cost of labour materials or overhead expenses in carrying out the Company's obligations under this Agreement (of the existence and amount of which increases the certificate of the Secretary or other authorised official of the Company shall be conclusive evidence) or in the event of the imposition of new taxes or the revising of existing taxes the Company shall be entitled to make an increase in the Annual Charge payable hereunder (whether or not such Charge has been paid in advance) such increase to come into effect (when notification to an official body may be required) on the date such notification becomes effective or (when no such notification is required) on the day appointed by the Company whereupon the amount of such increase as applies to the unexpired balance of any period in respect of which any Annual Charge has been paid in advance shall become immediately due and payable

This masterpiece from a council rent book works differently from many of the pieces in this book. You may think you understand it. But read it again. If you are responsible for painting your front door, can you pay someone else to do it for you?

Wherever the tenant is responsible under this agreement for doing or not doing something, he or she is also responsible for ensuring that nobody else does or not do, that particular thing.

Anyone considering early retirement would be well advised to look at the small print of their pension plan before handing in their notice. If it's anything like this, they'll probably reach pension age before they work it out:

NOTWITHSTANDING ANYTHING HEREIN CONTAINED TO THE CONTRARY THE VALUE OF THE POLICY AT A RETIREMENT DATE EARLIER THAN THE MATURITY DATE SHALL BE ASCERTAINED AT THE RETIREMENT DATE (HEREINAFTER REFERRED TO IN THIS ENDORSEMENT AS THE "REDUCED SUM"(SECURED BY THE PREMIUMS PAID IN RESPECT OF THIS INCREASE PRIOR TO THAT DATE, IN ACCORDANCE WITH THE SOCIETY'S RATES IN FORCE AT THE DATE HEREOF, AND ADDING TO THE REDUCED SUM THE REVERSIONARY BONUSES ATTACHING TO THE POLICY IN RESPECT OF THIS INCREASE REDUCED IN THE PROPORTION WHICH THE REDUCED SUM BEARS TO THE UNDERMENTIONED INCREASE IN THE SUM ASSURED.

Local authority planning departments need vision and a long-term perspective. Perhaps, in the long term, this will become crystal clear:

"If by 03.04.89 you have not received notification that your application is invalid and the Authority dealing with your application have not given you notice of their decision, and you have not agreed with them in writing that the period within which their decision shall be given may be extended you may appeal to the Secretary of State in accordance with Sections 36 and 37 of the Town and Country Planning Act 1971 by notice sent within six months from that date, unless the application has already been referred by the Authority to the Secretary of State for the Environment. Appeals must be made on a form which is obtainable from the Secretary of State for the Environment."

One of the joys of gobbledygook is the happy juxtaposition of the incomprehensible with the blindingly obvious. Two sentences from a car manufacturer's document illustrate this to perfection:

'Clause C. Unless the Dealer being appointed is a new entrant to the distribution system or we are required by law or by special agreement to pay "appropriate compensation upon termination," the termination notice period for an agreement of indefinite duration must be at least one year for both parties (or, if a fixed-term agreement, the term must be at least four years). One year has been interpreted to mean 12 months.'

Utter Drivel!

With many writers of gobbledygook it's not just what they say that's at fault, they also say far too much. Try this for 'sighs':

13. Purchaser's Default. In the event that the Purchaser defaults in the payment of any installment of purchase price, taxes, insurance, interest, or the annual charge described elsewhere herein, or shall default in the performance of any other obligations set forth in this Contract, the Seller may: at his option: (a) Declare immediately due and payable the entire unpaid balance of purchase price, with accrued interest, taxes, and annual charge, and demand full payment thereof, and enforce conveyance of the land by termination of the contract or according to the terms hereof, in which case the Purchaser shall also be liable to the Seller for reasonable attorney's fees for services rendered by any attorney on behalf of the Seller, or (b) sell said land and premises or any part thereof at public auction, in such manner, at such time and place, upon such terms and conditions, and upon such public notice as the Seller may deem best for the interest of all concerned, consisting of advertisement in a newspaper of general circulation in the county or city in which the security property is located at least once a week for Three (3) successive weeks or for such period as applicable law may require and, in case of default of any purchaser, to re-sell with such postponement of sale or resale and upon such public notice thereof as the Seller may

determine, and upon compliance by the Purchaser with the terms of sale, and upon judicial approval as may be required by law, convey said land and premises in fee simple to and at the cost of the Purchaser, who shall not be liable to see to the application of the purchase money; and from the proceeds of sale: First to pay all proper costs and charges, including but not limited to court costs, advertising expenses, auctioneer's allowance, the expenses, if any, required to correct any irregularity in the title, premium for Seller's bond, auditor's fee, attorney's fee, and all other expenses of sale incurred in and about the protection and execution of this contract, and all moneys advanced for taxes, assessments, insurance, and with interest thereon as provided herein, and all taxes due upon said land and premises at time of sale, and to retain as compensation a commission of five percent (5%) on the amount of said sale or sales; SECOND, to pay the whole amount then remaining unpaid of the principal of said contract, and interest thereon to date of payment, whether the same shall be due or not, it being understood and agreed that upon such sale before maturity of the contract the balance thereof shall be immediately due and payable; THIRD, to pay liens of record against the security property according to their priority of lien and to the extent that funds remaining in the hands of the Seller are available; and LAST, to pay the remainder of said proceeds, if any, to the vendor, his heirs, personal representatives, successors or assigns upon the delivery and surrender to the vendee of possession of the land and premises, less costs and excess of obtaining possession.

And *that* is one easy-to-read 513-word sentence. By comparison, the Plain English Campaign recommends an average sentence length of 15-25 words to make any text easy to read.

This sentence in a mortgage agreement from New Zealand is much shorter – a flimsy 236 words. But then again, it has no semicolons, no colons and no commas from beginning to end:

Any demand or notice required hereunder or authorised by the Property Law Act 1952 or by this mortgage to be served on the Mortgagor shall be in writing (which shall be sufficiently authenticated if signed by the Mortgagee or any person acting for or on behalf of or under the express or implied authority of the Mortgagee) and may be served on the Mortgagor by being delivered personally or by being left on any part of the said land or by posting the same by prepaid registered letter addressed to the Mortgagor at his place of abode or business last known to the Mortgagee and any such mode of service shall be valid effectual and sufficient notwithstanding that at the date of such service the Mortgagor to the knowledge of the Mortgagee or otherwise may be lunatic dead bankrupt in liquidation or absent from New Zealand or shall not have received the same and notwithstanding any other matter or event whatsoever and if any such demand or notice shall have been left on any part of the said land such demand or notice shall be deemed to have been served on the same day or if posted as aforesaid shall be deemed to have been served when the letter would in the ordinary course of post have been delivered and the receipt of the Post Office for a registered letter so addressed shall be conclusive evidence of service.

Personally, we rather like the idea that it's still OK to send a 'demand or notice' to someone even if you know they 'may be lunatic dead bankrupt in liquidation or absent from New Zealand'. If it does mean that ...

As a means of informing the greatest number of people in the simplest way, the press release has much to commend it. Unfortunately the system runs into problems when the message is written like this:

'b) the basis of refund is not pro rata but is the difference, if any, between:
i) the price paid for the season ticket, and
ii) the total cost of the appropriate combination of monthly and weekly, seven-day or five-day season tickets and full return tickets necessary to cover one return journey per day up to the date the season ticket was handed in, less an administrative charge.'

Utter Drivel!

If you are unsure about what schools are and what is happening in schools today, one 'human resource briefing paper' may hold the answers. On the other hand, it may not:

For many schools, the central principles of AIP are increasingly the cornerstone of school development. Enhanced autonomy for schools has thrown into even sharper focus than before the scale of resourcing represented by staffing and the consequent responsibility to ensure that this major resource is properly equipped to deliver quality education for the community.

If people want a job doing urgently, it is important to impress on them that you are the patient, methodical sort:

I refer to your telephone conversation with my assistant in which you ask if the Council can now proceed to provide two plugs for electricity supply purposes in the above premises pursuant to an inspection in that behalf which has been made you advise my assistant by the Council's officers. I understand that the two plugs are in order to provide a heating facility in the waiting room and a further one in the office part of the premises and that you are apprehensive that if steps are not taken quickly to implement the provision of these facilities some avoidable discomfort will be caused to persons using the offices. I am asking the Council's Chief Technical Officer to look into the question with a view to advising you direct of the Council's proposals pursuant to your present request.
I understand that there is provision for four plugs in all in the premises two of which are in use, and that the other two plugs now requested may be in situ but need repair or replacement.

The nature of time has puzzled physicists for centuries. It's pleasing to see that some government agencies are working hard to explain specific periods of time, even if no one else is able to share the fruits of their wisdom:

In accordance with Regulation 3(2) of the Social Security (Contributions) Regulations 1979, I hereby give notice to J. Bloggs, M. Bean, C. Chaplin, B. Keaton and Smith & Jones being the secondary contributor, that I am satisfied that the greatest part of the earnings paid to, or for the benefit of. The above employees in respect of employed earner's employment by Smith & Jones is normally paid at intervals of greater length that the shortest interval at which any part of such earnings are normally paid or treated as paid. Accordingly, the length of the earnings period for the purposes of payment of earnings related contributions shall hereafter be the length of that longer interval, that is to say, the earnings period shall be the period of quarterly.

Some things are better left unsaid and this regional health authority report proves it. The writer deserves particular praise for the tantalizing effect of the last sentence, which leaves the reader seeking ever-deeper truths and meanings:

This Outline Regional Information Strategy is an interim report. In a sense, an Information Strategy can never be definitive. To talk about information is to talk about objectives. A lot of thought is now being applied throughout the NHS to mission statements and objectives, from which we should obtain a clearer view of our information needs. However, objectives will never stand still, and therefore an Information Strategy will of necessity be a continuously developing concept. The process of clarification will be incremental, and the concept of a definitive strategy will remain illusory.

Reading the small print sometimes amounts to a crisis of personal identity. Try working your way through this to decide who is who and what he or she can or cannot do:

If and to the extent that any person by whom the Seller has been supplied with the goods supplied hereunder (hereinafter referred to as 'the Supplier' (validly excludes restricts or limits his liability to the Seller in respect of the said goods or of any loss or damage arising in connection therewith the liability of the Seller to the Buyer in respect of the said goods or of any loss or damage arising in connection therewith shall be correspondingly excluded restricted or limited.

The value of your pension can increase or decrease. Or both, maybe:

Where not more than 5 years' premiums remain to be paid or in the final 5 years to pension date (single premium contracts) our current practice is to enhance the transfer value by a proportion of the current rate of terminal bonus. The proportion increases with each decrease in the whole number of years to pension date.

People who use three words when one will do lurk behind some fine examples of gobbledygook. But compared with this answer to an inquiry about property insurance, they are masters of conciseness:

Property Insurance Regulations:

2 For the purposes of a Mortgage whether existing or new to which these Regulations are applied –

a) The provisions directly or indirectly concerning insurance of the Property contained in the Mortgage or in any Mortgage Conditions governing it shall have effect subject to and only so far as those provisions are operable consistently and concurrently with these Regulations;

b) Any obligation imposed or expressed to be imposed on the Society by the Mortgage or the Mortgage Conditions governing it shall be of no effect.

They then explain 2(a):

In answer to paragraph two of your letter, the regulation 2(a) states that the provisions contained in the Mortgage Conditions concerning insurance on the property will only be enforced if the borrower contravenes or does not comply with the Property Insurance Regulations.

and 2(b):

Paragraph two (b) of the Property Insurance Regulations 1982 form basically means that the Society waives its right to insure the property. The Society's right to insure is laid down in the Mortgage Conditions. However, upon completion by the borrower, the Regulation forms precede the obligation on the Society to insure, contained within the Mortgage Conditions.

Still baffled?

To clarify my explanation regarding paragraph two (b) of the Property Insurance Regulation forms, I would advise you that when the regulation forms are completed by the borrower, these regulations amend the Society's Mortgage Conditions to allow borrowers to arrange their own property insurance.

Could you just run that by me one more time?

With increased awareness of plain English, more and more government bodies are taking the trouble to make their documents reader-friendly. But judging by this mega-paragraph, there are still government bodies that have a fairly warped view of 'friendship':

"For the purposes of determining whether Paragraph 9 of Schedule 7A applies (or pursuant to Regulations 3(1) or 4(1) would apply) to a hereditament for a transitional day, the circumstances in which that paragraph is to be treated as applying to a hereditament for a preceding day by virtue of Paragraph 7 or 8 of that Schedule as described in sub-paragraph (1)*c) of those paragraphs include Regulation 3 applying to the hereditament for the preceding day, or the hereditament being a relevant hereditament for the purposes of Regulation 4 for that preceding day, by virtue of Paragraph 7 or 8 of that Schedule (as the case may be) as modified in effect by Regulations 3 and 4."

This extract comes from a leaflet about a conference on employee communications. If this is typical of the level of communications between bosses and workers, is it any wonder that British labour relations are called into question so often?

EVALUATING THE CHANGING ROLE OF COMMUNICATIONS IN FLATTER COMPANY STRUCTURES, ENSURING YOUR COMMUNICATIONS STRATEGY KEEPS UP TO DATE

including...

- Pinpointing the implications of a reduced number of layers for delivery combined with a reduced number of receivers of feedback
- Effectively using cross functional teams and matrix/project based teams in communications across organisational or functional boundaries

If you've paid in your first premium, we'll insure you, taking all the conditions of this agreement into account. In other words:

NOW THIS POLICY WITNESSETH that subject to the Conditions and Warranties included or endorsed herein and subject to the provisions, definitions, conditions, exclusions and exceptions applicable to the whole of the Policy or any Section thereof and subject also to any Memorandum or Warning contained in the Policy and the Insured having paid to the Head Office of the Company or Lucky Insurance Ltd the first premium for an insurance as hereinafter described for the period described in the Schedule, the Company severally promises and agrees with the said Insured his Executors and Administrators during the currency of this Policy to the insurance for Loss or Damage, or injury, or as specified in the Schedule, of the items in the Schedule.

Jargon, ambiguity and bad grammar are just some of the things that make writing a minefield of potential misunderstanding. The writer of the following banking gem made only one mistake, however – picking up his pen:

"The Principal Cardholder must repay at least 5% of the amount shown on the statement as outstanding or £5 (or the full amount (if less than £5), whichever is greater, within 25 days of the statement date (or, if the Bank considers that it is for any reason impossible or impractical to provide or send a statement, from the date determined by the Bank in accordance with Condition 18). Condition 4.)"

One of the engaging aspects of a lot of gobbledygook is its

creators' earnest desire to provide as much detailed information as they can. This letter from a government department shows what can happen when this sense of public service becomes too strong:

It is a well established principle that, in the absence of express words or necessary implication statutes do not bind the Crown. It is the Department's view that, to the extent that staff residences are Crown property (by virtue of the vesting of the freehold in the Secretary of State), they cannot be designated under section 5 of the 1988 Act. Designation under that section enables a collective community charge to be levied on a person with a qualifying interest in the designated dwelling. Those with qualifying interests are persons who either have the freehold interest (where there is no single leasehold interest) or have an interest in a lease or under lease which is not itself subject to a single inferior leasehold interest. In the case of properties to which you refer, the freehold will be vested in the Crown and it is unlikely that there will be a qualifying leasehold interest. Accordingly, and on the basis that the relevant provisions of the 1988 Act do not bind the Crown, there is unlikely to be any person in relation to those properties who is capable of being subject to a charging authority's collective community charge. It would not be appropriate for me to comment on the actions of the community charge registration officer in the absence of details of the particular case in question.

Want to cut down on irritating paperwork? Confuse millions? Be rude to your customers? Try putting this at the bottom of your electricity bills:

For office use, please do not deface

Bill graffiti artists beware ...

Utter Drivel!

In attempting to cast light on what he or she clearly saw as a cause of confusion, the writer of this piece of company correspondence added a new meaning to 'class struggle':

There is an unavoidable conflict of terminology in naming the Class and Instantiation. Instantiation is not itself a real instance but a class (namely, the class of all real instances). Likewise, Class is not a class of real instances but a class of classes (namely, the class of all classes of real instances). Instantiation could be renamed Class and Class renamed Type to avoid this. In that case the members of Class would not be classes and the members of Type would not be types.

'Montague' grammar is a semantic theory for natural language that endeavours to encompass indexical expressions and opaque contexts within an extensional theory by constructing set-theoretic representations of the intention of an expression in terms of functions of possible words. One can only guess whether the author of the following holds to that theory, but the evidence suggests that he or she may have had a hand in drafting the rules:

3 This appliance must be grounded. Connect only to properly grounded outlet. See "GROUNDING INSTRUCTIONS" found on next page.

Grounding Instruction

This appliance must be ground. In the event of an electrical short circuit, grounding reduces the risk of electric shock by providing an escape wire for the electric current. This appliance is equipped with a cord having a grounding wire with a grounding plug. The plug must be plugged into an outlet that is properly installed and grounded.

Certain insecure or paranoid people want to be insured when travelling abroad. Tread Carefully Travel Insurance Ltd have developed a fine technique for refusing them:

We thank you for your letter of the 3rd March 1981 advising us of the School Group travelling to Holland on a five day tour.

We would advise that our policy does exclude a contingency consequent upon a condition which is receiving or awaiting treatment at the date of issue of the policy.
We would therefore advise that the person who had the heart operation in 1963 is not receiving any of the forementioned as she will be covered for that condition under the policy. If the lady is receiving any of the aforementioned the policy only excludes her for a contingency consequent upon that particular condition. We still wish to offer her the cover of the rest of the policy including medical and other expenses and cancellation or curtailment due to any other unforeseen condition for which she is not receiving any medication or treatment for.
We hope this clarifies the situation.

When is a 'call' not a 'call', you may ask. The answer lies in this 'important notice' – somewhere:

IMPORTANT NOTICE
Attached is your schedule of calls for renewal of premium.

Please note that due to a new system, the first call will be on or within seven days of the renewal date of your policy, but the last call for this years premium will be one month before expiry date.

This differs to last year when the first call was at the beginning of the following month and the last call at the beginning of the month of expiry of your policy.

Consequently two calls may be made in one month.

Utter Drivel!

If you can't actually improve your traffic system, reach for your dictionary. A local authority here takes the lead in language development:

Line 5. Delete 'Bottlenecks', insert 'Localized Capacity Deficiencies'.

Common Traffic Problems Number 4: Localized Steering Deficiency

Electoral registers by their nature are concerned with events destined to take place in the future. Perhaps this is the reason why some letters refuse even to admit the existence of a past tense:

If you are living at your present address since before 11th October last year then it is likely that you are registered for your present address. In that case just write "as above".

Is it any wonder that international espionage fell out of favour in the 1990s? When the Maastricht Treaty appeared secret codes became obsolete. Even in a document of such rich potential, article 41.1 manages to be outstanding:

Simplified amendment procedure

41.1. In accordance with Article 106(5) of this Treaty, Articles 5.1, 5.2, 5.3, 17, 18, 19.1, 22, 23, 24, 26, 32.2, 32.3 32.4, 32.6, 33.1(a) and 36 of this Statute may be amended by the Council, acting either by a qualified majority on a recommendation from the ECB and after consulting the Commission, or unanimously on a proposal from the Commission and after consulting the ECB.

And after reading the 1967 Companies Act, nobody can doubt that British parliamentary drafting is as thorough as anything the EC can produce:

Subsections (4), (5) and (6) of the last foregoing section shall, with the substitution, for references to that section, of references to this section, apply for the purposes of this section as they apply for the purposes of that section.

'Say what you mean' is one of the golden rules of plain English. You would have thought that 'I can't help you but here is a leaflet that can' would be a simple message, but not for the writer of this classic waffle:

Thank you for your letter requesting information to be disclosed to you under the provisions of Section 129 of the Land Registration Act 1925 ("the Section").

I would draw to your attention that the Land Registration (Open Register) Rules 1990, which came into force on 3 December 1990, makes the information you are seeking now available using Form 109. There is thus no need to invoke the Section which was enacted to enable information previously not available to the public to be passed to certain Authorities.

The Section will of course continue to be available but generally a request for information under this section will now only be considered where the information is not accessible under the Land Registration (Open Register) Rules 1990 although there may be other exceptional circumstances which would also justify an application under the section. Each application for information under the Section will therefore now be considered on its individual merits having regard to the points I have made above. In your present application (in the case of the applications made under cover of your letter) I have to say that the information will not be made available under the Section although that decision does not affect your right to apply under the Land Registration (Open Register) Rules 1990.

If you are unfamiliar with the open register the Land Registry produces a leaflet (Explanatory Leaflet 15) which sets out in an elementary manner what information is available under the Open Register Rules and how to complete Form 109. ~~(I am enclosing a copy for your information)~~. (A copy of this leaflet will be sent upon request).

~~Why can't you send me the leaflet?~~ Thank you for being so helpful ...

For authors of situation comedy, there are vacancies – in the electricity business ...

Dear Sir/Madam

INTER-QUARTERLY COLLECTION ACCOUNTS

Due to the recent tariff increases it is necessary to empty certain meters which are liable to reach the 'full box' situation before the quarter ends.

For reasons explained above, a collector will visit your home on 10 February 1983. I would appreciate your co-operation in availing the collector access to your meter. If your meter remains unemptied there is a risk that your meter will be full before the due quarterly collection resulting in a 'no lights' situation.

and in banking ...

Dear Madam

With reference to my recent letter I note that your account is still £33.93 overdrawn. In view of the time which has elapsed I shall be most grateful if you will regularise this out of order situation.

It's always reassuring to know why people take the trouble to write letters. The director of one local authority technical services division offered an explanation:

This letter is written on behalf of the Council acting as Estate owner and/or as the party entitled to enforce Estate Covenants affecting the above-mentioned property, and refers only to consideration of the application under Estate Covenant control.

Utter Drivel!

Housing associations feature in this report from a city council in the north-west of England. How they feature is a matter for debate:

In many areas it is unlikely that successful housing renewal programmes can be implemented without increasing the viability of housing association rehabilitation, and in recognising the contribution that housing associations can make particularly in area based programmes, the priority which should be provided when an area is declared should be reflected in an enhancement of housing association funding for rehabilitation.

Studying this foreign language textbook is cleverly made to seem like child's play after reading the preface:

There is a grammar and syntax of ideas as well as one of words and phrases. Yet while the efforts of teachers and authors regularly converge on the latter, they are rarely directed at creating a coherent and constructive approach to the former, least of all where the divergences of conceptual models as between languages are most crucial, i.e. in areas of linguistic specialisation relating to many central transactions of social communication: politics, economics, science and technology, commerce, sociology and so on. Given appropriate material, however, in the form of extended passages of representative writing from such areas and appropriate written exercises, students can learn to adopt its specific 'forma mentis'. Such a training will in turn enable them both to function effectively within the 'communications system' of the foreign language and if necessary to produce authentic translations into their own in important registers (see Note on Language Registers on p.5) usually neglected and therefore impenetrable.

At least it ends on the right note …

These instructions have an admirably carefree attitude to building a chair:

Assemble the single parts (see picture) following nrs 1-2-3. Insert the wheels in the prepared holes in the base. If the wheels are provided with filletted pins, screw them.

What adds to the entertainment in this example is trying to

work out what precisely is being assembled:

- Jointer (1) with white-mark handhold (2) on firebowl (10) hold-screw the bearing lifter should be shown in front.
- then the legs (3) in jointer (2) insert with screw (4) fasten and fix
- after the ready-set of toolside (5) strike together the collecting dish (6) put in
- Please the handle of the blunt side of cricket chirps, and fasten the clinch and put in the complete cricket crips.
- in order not to shake the firebowl, the handle should be loosen.

While studying gobbledygook for fifteen years, the Plain English Campaign has spotted certain features which crop up again and again. One law of gobbledygook, demonstrated by this document, states that the more important the document, the fewer the people who will be able to understand it.

The hirer may only terminate this contract during the minimum period of hire by notice given in accordance with paragraph 14 because of an increase in the rate of rental which (whether alone or cumulatively with any other increase in a period not exceeding 12 months of the term of this contract) has the effect of increasing the rate of rental initially payable by a percentage greater than the percentage increase of the Retail Price Index last published before the notification of the increase to the hirer in accordance with this contract over the

Retail Price Index last published before the beginning of the minimum period of hire.

Sometimes a writer is so successful that even doctors cannot understand the document. When this happened in Devon, the Doctor Confusion Committee quickly clarified the situation:

In August the Department issued an amendment to the Statement of Allowances (S29) setting out the arrangements for payment of new rates of contraceptive service fees, payable in respect of quarterly payments due after 1.4.79. It has now come to the notice of the Department that the amendment has not been interpreted by all Doctor Confusion Committees in the way that was intended. A review has had to be undertaken in respect of payments made following the issue of the amendment.

The intention of paragraph 3 of SA29 was that except for claims submitted late, all claims in the count on 1st April 1979 including claims first counted on 1st July 1978 or later, should be paid at the new rate (i.e. the 1st April 1979 rate) until the termination of the life of the claim. In the case of a claim submitted late this should be dealt with as if it had been submitted on time. This means that payment should be at the old rate (i.e. the 1st April 1978 rate) for the number of quarters the claim would have been in the count up to and including 1st January 1979 had it been submitted on time and payment should be at the new rate for only the remaining number of quarters of its life.

If borrowers ever questioned how they were perceived in the eyes of their lenders, this life-mortgage policy, in which they take on at least half-a-dozen identities, should leave them in no doubt:

If "the Mortgagor" shall consist of two or more parties such expressions shall throughout mean and include such two or more parties and each of them or (as the case may require) such two or more parties or any of them and shall so far as the context admits be construed as well in the plural as in the singular and all covenants assignments charges agreements and undertakings herein expressed or implied on the part of the Mortgagor shall be deemed to be joint and several covenants assignments charges agreements and undertakings by such parties and in particular this security and the covenant in clause 1 hereof and the remaining covenants assignments charges agreements and undertakings herein contained shall extend and apply to any moneys owing or liabilities incurred by any of such parties to the Bank whether solely or jointly with each other or with any other person and references to the Mortgagor in relation to the retirement of bills and in clause 4, 9, 10 and 12 shall mean and include any one or more of such parties as well as such parties jointly.

If you are now wondering about the role of the human being in our increasingly machine-dominated world, this engaging description should help you out:

Non-automatic weighing instruments

Coverage: non-automatic weighing instruments, that is measuring instruments which determine the mass of a body or other mass-related magnitudes, quantities, parameters or characteristics by using the action of gravity, and which require the intervention of an operator.

One of the charms of English is its ability to absorb a constant flow of new words. It remains to be seen whether the creative powers of the assembly instructions for this Japanese aeroplane will make a lasting contribution to the language:

Check if Tail Fine is complete pendicularity. Be in same length A-A. Also be in same length B-B. Take measurements exactly.

It's reassuring to find insurance companies doing their bit to reduce the volume of traffic on our roads. Motor insurance documents which open like this are a sure way of weeding out all but the most determined drivers even before they get behind the wheel:

The undernamed having proposed for insurance in respect of the Motor Vehicle described in the Schedule below, the risk is hereby held covered in terms of the Company's usual form of Policy applicable thereto with the alterations indicated, for the period shown, unless the cover be terminated by the Company by notice in writing, in which case the insurance will thereupon cease and a proportionate part of the annual premium otherwise applicable for such insurance will be charged for the time the Company has been on risk.
This temporary Cover Note is not evidence of an annual contract or that the insurer will enter into an annual contract.

Probing academics exercise their minds by studying the world's great mysteries: the Pyramids, Stonehenge, the disappearance of the dinosaurs. But anyone looking for a real challenge might care to try this product description for part of an electric drill:

Suction hood

Major aspiration capacity for particular working exigencies.

One of the basic principles of insurance is that the person with the policy should take good care of their property. And you are almost certain to do so after contemplating making an insurance claim with the company which wrote this:

Any item which covers articles not separately specified is subject to the following special conditions of average, that is to say, if the value of all articles covered by such item shall at the time of any loss or damage be greater than the value of the sum insured hereby in respect thereof, the Insured shall be entitled to recover hereunder only such proportion of the said loss or damage as the sum insured in respect of such item bears to the total value of all articles covered by such item.

When it comes to understanding how investment payments are calculated, most of us faced with explanations like this would feel more confident predicting the first winner of the National Lottery:

Each recurring accumulation contribution in respect of an Arrangement will be equal in amount to the initial level of recurring accumulation contribution in respect of that Arrangement (included in the overall initial level of recurring accumulation contribution advised to the Member)

Utter Drivel!

The writers of this membership form have invented a device for wrecking perfectly clear sentences. They simply attach a landmine at the end:

Full Membership covers the Full Member, his children aged 17 or under and one of the following relations living in the same household: wife, husband, daughter, son, mother, father, brother, sister (inclusive).

So you want someone else to do your job? You have to understand this first:

We consider only work that is normally carried out by an insured to be work that is capable of delegation and not work that is of a different nature from that they carry out.

In these days of increasingly caring, responsible councils you can expect to receive clear and informative letters of the very highest order. You can expect it, but as this letter from one county council shows, you won't always get it:

It would appear from the response so far that the section in the Notes of Guidance headed Employment Details has been misinterpreted. The volume of records to be input required a decision to be taken to commence computer records from a point in time hence the notional start on your print may indicate January or September 1988 if you were in post at that time. The computer will therefore not hold any historical appointments other than the employment operative at the time of input. Again, I acknowledge this may not have been the first appointment with the Authority or the correct start date for the first appointment shown on the print but all historical information will still be retained on manual records for reference purposes. I trust this will allay any fears about historical information not being retained on the computer.

One advantage of the memorandum is that the writer can feel confident that he or she is using a common language to address colleagues who are working to achieve similar ends. But then again, maybe not:

In examining the intended profile for the post of Information Officer the union has been mindful of the residual posts of Organising Assistant the duties and responsibilities attaching thereto and the range of support now required to both the service group and functional elements of the regional structure. With the exception of the IT User Support responsibility within the aforementioned profile and the function of Committee Administration historically embraced by the Organising Assistant remit (both of which would demand specific provision within the administrative resource) it is considered the better option that posts of Organising Assistant (or similar designation) be retained and that an appropriate job profile be designed: this to include items (i) – (iv) in the Information Officer profile and the requirement of generic support to the staffing and lay structures established. In these circumstances I am recommending that a post of Information Officer not be determined at this time and that the requisite number of Organising Assistant posts be reviewed.

Utter Drivel!

If you were ever in any doubt about the changing role of the police, this extract from a police communication and consultation briefing pack provides reassurance:

there will be no systematic fragmentation of the provisioning departments for co-location on areas, rather, a matrix of provider/customer (purchaser) relationships will be developed, incorporating aspects of service delivery level agreements.

Sometimes it is necessary to let the ratepayers know that they are all repulsive microbes or common criminals, like this London council:

The Council's policy is that bona fide residents only are entitled to parking contracts at the very much reduced rates which you enjoy. The test of residence is the same as that applied to applicants for on-street residents' parking permits.

As I do not have any recent proof of residence at the above address I must therefore ask you to furnish me with documentary proof of your usual place of abode. Normally a letter from your landlord or agent will suffice.

Pending clarification of your residential status to the Council's satisfaction I am afraid it will not be possible to renew your current resident's parking contract when it expires.

If a 'top-up' loan is what you're after, look no further than 'Life and Death Insurance':

I hereby give you notice pursuant to the terms of the mortgage deed regulating your Top-up loan with 'Life and Death' that, with effect from 1st February 1990 (and until further notice), the rate of interest payable on your said Top-up loan in terms of the said mortgage deed will be 2.5% above the 'Life and Death' Home Loan Rate as it shall vary from time to time in lieu of the rate of interest therein stated. The said mortgage deed provides for interest to be paid at a reduced rate namely 1.5% above the 'Life and Death' Home Loan Rate on punctual payment.

Repetition is a basic component of this civil servant's style:

Where a married woman's own contribution record is not sufficient to give her a retirement pension basic component at the standard rate, her basic component may be increased by the amount of basic component to which she is entitled on her husband's contributions, subject to the combined basic component not exceeding the standard rate of basic component payable to a married woman on her husband's contributions.

Knowing your rights is one thing, exercising them is quite a different matter, particularly when you get a letter like this explaining what is and isn't allowed:

Regulation 4 of the Child Support Appeal Tribunal (Procedure) Regulations 1992 provides that where the Chairman of the Tribunal is satisfied that the Tribunal does not have jurisdiction to entertain a purported appeal he may make a declaration to that effect and such declaration shall dispose of the purported appeal.

We have to give full marks to the building society manager we've quoted here. Not only did he compliment an account holder for paying by standing order, he managed to offer her a pension in such a way that she probably didn't even know he was angling for more business:

I am pleased to note that you add to the benefits of your account by the means of regular payments by standing order. You will note now no doubt not even miss the amount from use of your bank account such is the discipline and habit of this saving.

Then after suggesting she take out a pension with the building society: he ends on an encouraging note:

Without doubt the compound advantageous effect early start to such plans mean that the earlier the better if you can take part.

As if making a profit wasn't hard enough, some of the guidance from the tax people makes enjoying that profit even more demanding:

If the profits for either year do not exceed seven-tenths of the profits of the other (or are nil), the profits for each year are adjusted to half the total of both. If either year's profits exceed seven-tenths of the other's but are less than three-quarters, the profits are adjusted by adding to the lower and subtracting from the higher the amount obtained by multiplying the difference by three and deducting three-quarters of the higher figure. (Thus, if the profits are £21,900 and £30,000, the adjusted profits after relief would be £23,700 and £28,200.)

The English language can be full of traps. For instance, when we refer to a 'small businessman' do we mean an ordinary-sized man with a small business, or a small man with an ordinary-sized business? One way round pitfalls like this is to follow the example set by this domino guide and write your instructions in another language:

His heibour leftward has to ask between his plates such that in one of its halfs has the same number of dots as the first plate laying on the table, i.e. 6:5 or 6:4.

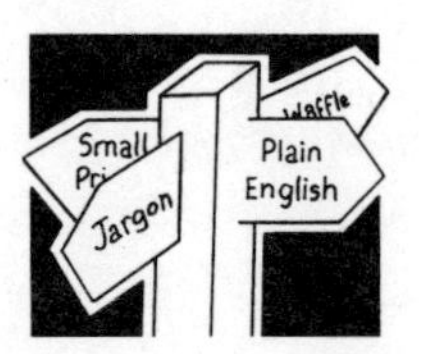

In the commercial world, good customer relations lie at the heart of a company's success. Well intentioned as this letter is, it somehow fails to achieve the desired effect:

Further to my recent correspondence I am writing to confirm that the delivery and installation date of your new Shed Unit is scheduled for the 3rd June.
I am sorry for any inconvenience caused and confirm that our delivery lee times do take place from the point at which the order becomes fully paid and I note that the above order was receipted by ourselves on the 4th April. I would apologise for any undue inconvenience caused in your not being able to contact our Customer Service telephone number and confirm that there is every wish to make you a satisfied customer and with this action now taken I am sure that this can be brought about shortly. I am sure you will gain many years use and

satisfaction from this new unit and I would assure you of our continuing attention.

Utter Drivel!

This United Phone Lines telex has found a novel way of saying do nothing for now:

IT WOULD BE USEFUL IF UNITED PHONE LINES SCOTLAND AND OTHER REGIONS RECEIVING COPIES OF THIS TELEX COULD MAINTAIN A TEMPORIZING STANCE WITH MINIMAL EXTENSION OF THE CURRENT SUBPOSTMASTER 'E' LISTING UNTIL A MORE COMPETENT GENERAL PROVISION CAN BE MADE TO COVER THE REQUIREMENTS OF ALL CUSTOMERS.

This explanation by the International Sickness Service (ISS) has hidden depths. You have to read it twice to appreciate just how much you don't understand it:

3. Service which counts for the purpose of calculating the 'notional' pension is optant service with an ISS employing authority (including Scotland, Northern Ireland or the Isle of

Man) the civil service or local government. If there is a break of 12 months or more between optant employments then the earlier service cannot reckon.

Suffering the torment of piles? This package leaflet offers immediate relief:

A non-greasy, water-miscible cream with a marked anti-pruritic and analgesic action. The special base achieves intimate contact with moist surfaces, has a drying effect on exudative skin conditions and is particularly suitable for application to exposed surfaces.

Modern communications generally make it easier to do things and moving money about is no exception. On the other hand, look at this for a failed transmission:

A money transmission service account means an account which is provided by a society to a person to facilitate the provision of money transmission services by the society to that person and on which that person may, temporarily or occasionally, in the course of and incidental to receiving money transmission services from the society, become indebted to the society.

If there are mistakes in a document, let the readers sort them out for themselves. This council shows the way in the 'Great Bullville Street Local (District) Plan – Consultation Plan':

Erratum. Page 19: Shopping Facilities. For the justification statement read the implementation note and vice versa.

Utter Drivel!

Persuading people to part with their money has never been easy, but this scheme which appears to offer the chance of quick riches has to be a winner. If the reader hasn't gone into a coma by the end of it, he or she will probably sign up quite happily to be spared any more letters like this one:

Would you like to receive £145?
If the answer is YES, then read on.
The Get Rich Quick Club returns £300 for each £55 entry paid

over 3 transactions of £100. This is generated by entries increasing and perpetuating the cash-flow within the Club controlled by the computer system. Members pay a once only £30 registration fee and then purchase at least 1 entry per month ensuring a constant growth in the system. Each monthly entry will return £300 as above.

Sounds like hogwash to us.

Shareholders confronted with a fifteen-line addition to their company's rules were left scratching their heads when they tried to figure out what their board of directors had in mind:

"To lend money to any corporation, company, association, firm, body or person on such terms as may be thought fit and with or without security and to enter into any guarantee, contract of indemnity or suretyship and in particular (without limiting the generality of the foregoing) to guarantee, provide indemnities in respect of, support or secure, with or without consideration and whether by personal covenant or by mortgaging or charging all or any part of the Company's undertaking, property and assets (present and future) and its uncalled capital, or by all or any of such methods, the performance of the obligations of and the repayment or payment of the principal amounts of, and any premiums, interest and dividends on, any shares or other securities or borrowed monies of any corporation, company, association, firm, body or person including (without limiting the generality of the foregoing) any company which for the time being is a subsidiary or a holding company of the Company or another subsidiary of a holding company of the Company or is otherwise associated with the Company"."

Dealing in shares on the basis of information that has not been made public has been in the news frequently in the last ten years. But when share offers are presented in this way, it comes as a surprise that any shares are traded at all, legally or otherwise:

Other distributions in respect of Shares
Subject to provisions dealing with fractional entitlements, legal title to any non-cash distribution (other than Shares being issued in lieu of a cash dividend) made by the Company to the Custodian Bank or its nominee as the registered holder of Shares will normally be retained by the Custodian Bank and transferred by it to the relevant Purchasers after payment of the final instalment subject to the Purchasers paying any stamp duty or SDRT in connection with such transfer and to such arrangements as may be agreed by HM Treasury, the Company and the Custodian Bank. Purchasers at the time when such a distribution is made to the Custodian Bank may, as a result, have to satisfy a tax liability before they receive the transfer.

These planners in London don't wish to sound over-confident:

It is considered that further investigations should be carried out into this property before a recommendation could be made to Committee concerning the possibility of undertaking a feasibility study.

One way of making sure customers keep buying your product is to give it a short working life. With light bulbs and many mechanical products this is probably quite easy. Woollen sweaters pose more of a problem, but washing instructions in pidgin English help:

This article was treated against the contraction it can be washed at hand and it will conserve its form and beauty if was considered next greetings.

TO WASH: Invert the piece. Wash it in tepid water (40°C). Do not make white. Dissolve the detergent before the washing.

TO RINSE: Employ tepid water to eliminate the residues of soap or detergent.

TO PRESS: Press lightly without twist, or to utilise an hidro extractor. Take the shape at piece in the original dimension and dry it upon a plane area and without sun's action and highs temperatures.

TO STARCH: Utilise in preference to an iron of steam or to starch on a humid cloth.

Holding prospective policy holders in suspense even before they have signed the policy and paid the first premium is an unusual tactic. This company uses it to great effect with the question:

Do you require cover in respect of the following? (See overleaf)

A press release from Repeated Methods Ltd trumpets its message with such enthusiasm you feel almost obliged to applaud, without having a clue what commercial success you are acknowledging:

Repeated Methods Ltd today announced that it has grown exponentially in 1992, and that this accelerating rate of adoption has firmly established their Fractal Transform technology as a de-facto standard for still image compression.

Many officials are prone to repetition, but few can rival this insurance document in which variations on one word appear seven times in only six lines:

In accordance with section 52(2) of the Insurance Companies Act 1982 you are hereby notified that on 5 August 1992 Bullrush Ltd ("the transferor") and Bullrush Universal ("the transferee") executed an instrument of transfer whereby the transferor transferred to the transferee all the rights and obligations under the policies specified in the instrument of transfer.

There's something of an identity crisis locked inside this sales document:

"In the event of the goods being sold by the buyer in such manner as to pass a third party a valid title to the goods, whilst any such sums are due as aforesaid, the buyer shall be the Trustee for us of the proceeds of such sale or to the claim for such proceeds and the buyer shall place such proceeds in a separate account. Nothing herein shall constitute the buyer or our Agent for the purpose of any sub-sale.'

This council bows to the permissive age:

During the early days of public park provision the layout was very formal and grand, this traditional design has over the years changed mainly due to the cost and maintenance of this type of layout. The approach nowadays is one of providing informal areas, trees and grass. Formal bedding is made at focal points.

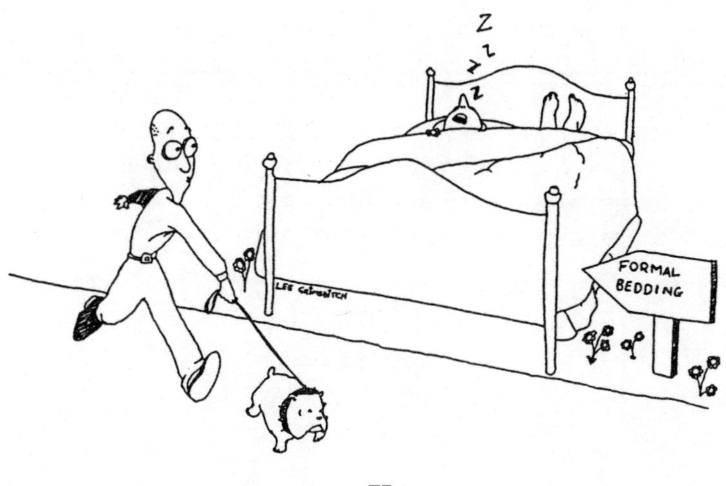

Civil servants are renowned for exercising great care in their writing. One government department certainly makes sure there is virtually no chance of anyone understanding their documents (and they're asking us to provide 'comprehensible information'!):

(1) Every employer and every self-employed person shall ensure that the employer of any employees from an outside undertaking who are working in his undertaking is provided with comprehensible information on –

(a) the risks to those employees' health and safety arising out of or in connection with the conduct by that first-mentioned employer or by that self-employed person of his undertaking; and

(b) the measures taken by that first-mentioned employer or by that self-employed person in compliance with the requirements and prohibitions imposed upon him by or under the relevant statutory provisions insofar as the said requirements and prohibitions relate to those employees.

(2) Paragraph (1) shall apply to a self-employed person who is working in the undertaking of an employer or a self-employed person as it applies to employees from an outside undertaking who are working therein; and the reference in that paragraph to the employer of any employees from an outside undertaking who are working in the undertaking of an employer or a self-employed person and the references in the said paragraph to employees from an outside undertaking who are working in the undertaking of an employer or a self-employed person shall be construed accordingly.

Even shopping doesn't spare us from gobbledygook. As we set off on longer and longer shelf-safaris, jargon and double-speak are never far away. Look at this helpful sign from a poultry section:

'Eviscerated without giblets' means the giblets have been removed.

When in doubt, or just wanting to inspire some, try out your trusted legal Latin:

Your attention is drawn to Conditions printed on the reverse side of the above agreement whereby the Caesar Electrical Corporation may determine the hiring thereunder by service of a notice upon you if (inter alia) any monthly payment or part thereof remains unpaid after the same shall have become due.

Many official replies avoid telling you what you really want to know. One from a London neighbourhood services department not only fails to provide answers, it actually raises a number of questions: Who wrote it? What language did he or she use? How did he or she get the job in the first place?

Repayment of Housing Benefit

From 14/12/92 to 20/12/92 you get 46.67 less than you did before.
46.67 per week X 1 Week(s) = 46.67

***This is not a recoverable overpayment so you are not being asked to repay this amount.

This means the amount to pay back is now 46.67.

Some manufacturers are so enthusiastic about a unified market throughout Europe that they have developed an all-purpose Euro-language for the benefit of their customers:

When you mount the cookerhood on a modulated kitchen please care that the superior border of the calibre is on the inferior border of the incorporated board;
When you fix the cookerhood to the incorporated board, please set this border on the wall upon the bottom of the incorporated board et use the un-hooped holes.

With the problem of unemployment a national concern, it is reassuring to see that some agencies still follow their own distinctive method of providing jobs:

"The engagement or use by a Client of a Temporary Worker or former Temporary Worker(s) introduced by the agency whether for a definite or indefinite period, or the introduction of such Temporary Worker(s) to other employers with a resulting engagement, renders the Client subject to the payment of an introduction fee calculated in accordance with the agency fees for permanent introductions, commencing gross taxable pay and taxable emoluments payable by the client to the worker concerned, provided that the engagement takes place within a period of 6 months from the termination of any temporary assignment."

By now you will have read enough bad writing to begin to feel confident about deciphering gobbledygook in its many forms. The introduction to the programme of Verona's 30th International Circus Festival might make you think again:

Many times I asks to myself if everything is permitted to the circus. Or, until what point is possible to experiment with dramaturgic materials typics of the circus to create a concectual product near at an astract vision of the circus. That's the point: the circus, if is possible a too easy comparation, if compared with the painting art, was during all his history a figurative art. Sometimes connected to a contemporary figurative or to a beautiful neoclassic, but too much times involved in a retoric scrap more artigianal than artistic.
The problem of the circus is at first its difficulty to evolve itself. It lives on stereotypes sometimes transforming it from art to simple artisanate (sometime of good taste). But if we except some cases, the circus stays there, lied at old schemas determining, with the time, a logic involution. There's the convintion (the false convintion), that the circus is the past, that the tradition have to be connected with the memory of our fathers and grandfathers and that will be dangerous to look for new ways. But the art, if it is creativity, doesn't have and cannot live of static schemas. It is moreover at the interior of these schemas that we have to search for new streets. I'm not affirming that the street of Centre National des Arts du Cirque is the new s way and the show that they presents in VeronaCirco '94 is the circus of the future, but it is sure that experiments like this one, right for their exageration, contributes to gives to the contemporary circus a renewed fisionomy, certainly auspicious to elevate it at pure art.

Some people liken members of the banking fraternity to rhinoceroses, because they're thick-skinned and charge a lot.

Unlike the rhino, though, it's not always easy to see their point, as this letter shows:

"Notwithstanding the aforesaid the manager shall not be obliged to buy or sell any Selected Range Investments in accordance with the instructions of the Investor if, in the manager's opinion, it is not reasonably practicable in accordance with its normal dealing practices to make such purchase or sale (taking account of other purchases or sales of the same investment required by the manager's other customers) at the relevant time in an amount or at a price considered by the manager to be satisfactory. The manager shall inform the Investor if any purchase or sale requested by such Investor is not made in full. Where a purchase or sale of a particular Selected Range Investment is required both by the Investor and other customers of the manager then, subject to compliance with the IMRO Rules, the manager shall have a complete discretion as to whether, and the extent to which, it shall exercise its power not to make or to scale down the purchase or sale requested by the Investor."

Who would have thought that the instructions for making a simple cup of herbal tea could provide such entertainment?

The exact preparation:
Hang the tea-bag in a cup and pour boiling water over it. Let draw 10 minutes in the covered cup. Then remove the tea-bag.

Add honey or sugar to taste.

Directions for use:
By experience one knows that medicinal herbs work best when drunk by small pulls. So after each pull a fair interval, without any haste. The proven action can still be fortified by regular drinking by way of cure.

In an attempt to clarify points of detail to their policy holders, some insurance companies go out of their way to provide explanations. When they do, a good many get themselves hopelessly lost, as this sample in the *Sunday Telegraph* illustrates:

"ANY lump sum paid in accordance with Provision 7 of the Second Schedule shall be an amount equal to the Basic Nominal Fund that would be applied to calculate the Alternative Annuity under Provision 5 or Provision 12 of the Second Schedule on the assumption that the Annuitant had elected under Provision 4 of the Second Schedule that the date of his death was the Alternative Vesting Date or if greater an amount equal to the premiums received by the Society."

Councillor Mark Brown, when leader of Bullville Council, set out the painful and unusual steps a fellow councillor was prepared to take to reach agreement with his striking employees:

There will be a further meeting of the negotiating body on or as near as possible to the 19th December to monitor this agreement and during the period to that date the Chairman of the Housing Committee will hold himself open and use his good offices to ensure that the spirit of this agreement is adhered to.

The typical writer worries whether to use 'infer' or 'imply', 'due to' or 'owing to', and 'confronted by' or 'confronted with'. The writer of this exercise in mass communication had no such anxieties. He appears to be concerned only to produce something as far from everyday English as possible:

Our new style reflects the optimism we, as an Association, now feel on behalf of medicine manufacturers. Improvements in the POM to P switch process have been key to creating a favourable regulatory framework for our industry. It is this backdrop that has enabled the Association to develop a pro-active strategy to "grow the market".

Utter Drivel!

Anyone starting out on this insurance document might well wonder precisely what they're letting themselves in for. 'Here, here!' their equally baffled friends may cry – but which 'here' they're referring to is anyone's guess:

Whereas the Insured herein named has by a signed proposal and declaration dated as herein stated which proposal and declaration the Insured has agreed shall be the basis of this Contract and be held as incorporated herein applied to the Insurers for insurance against the Insured Events specified in the Schedule hereto.

persons not . . . by this . . . the Mortgagor . . . person
, or affected by this . . . or make any . . .
for payment to or make any person or any transaction
udice to the liability of the Mortgagor or any person or any transaction
Principal or Mortgagor or any account or any the Law of
o any account or item of account or the Law of
, hereby also declared that Section 93 of the Law of
y and that the Mortgagor and his successors in title sha
at the same time redeeming every or any existing or fut
on other property now or at any time hereafter belong
to redeem any other such mortgage without at the san

The old maxim that you get what you pay for doesn't appear quite as reliable when you get to grips with the nitty-gritty of this home entertainment agreement:

Cloud 9 Sports will be provided by Cloud 9 Subscriber Services Limited as agent for British Cloud 9 Broadcasting Limited under the terms (except where inconsistent) of my existing subscription contract for the movie channel(s) so that references to the service include a reference to Cloud 9 Sports and the references to Subscription include a reference to the monthly fee above.

Except where inconsistent?

This public statement of a manufacturing company's environmental policy leaves a lingering doubt about what influence, if any, it has on the way the firm runs its business:

"Our **commitment** is to strive continuously to minimise adverse effects on the **environment** without compromising the high standards **customers** associate with our name"

Utter Drivel!

Town planners have hearts of gold. As alcoholism rises among visitors from Mars, they are even prepared to alter traffic systems to suit them:

Subject to banning right turning movements out of East Lane into King's Road ground level crossing facilities across King's Road, south of East Lane, could be provided by means of a staggered green man facility.

You might well think that this clause from a tenant's contract is rather long and impenetrable. You might well be right:

(4) At all times throughout the Lease to keep the premises insured against loss or damage by fire explosion lightning storm tempest flood burst pipes impact riot civil commotion aircraft and such other risks as the Council may reasonably require with insurers of repute under a policy noting the interest of the Lessee thereon in the full rebuilding cost approved by the Council including Architects and Surveyors fees and two years' loss of rent and to make all payments for the above purpose as soon as conveniently possible after the same shall become payable and to produce to the Lessee on demand details of the policy and premium last paid in respect thereof and to forthwith apply after any destruction or damage all moneys received by virtue of any such insurance in discharge of the cost and expense of and incidental to rebuilding and making good the destruction or loss in respect

of which the same shall have been received and to make up any deficiency out of its own monies PROVIDED that the Council's obligation under this covenant shall cease if the insurance shall be rendered void by reason of any act or default of the Lessee such reinstatement and making good being in all respects carried out in accordance with the then existing statutory provisions bye-laws and regulations affecting the same and in accordance with any planning approval which may be necessary PROVIDED HOWEVER that if the re-instatement of the premises or any part thereof shall be frustrated or proves impossible or impracticable all the insurance monies relating to such premises or part in respect of which it occurs (save that in respect of loss of rent) shall be divided between the Council and the Lessee in the proportions which the value of their respective interests in the premises or that part thereof bear to one another at the time of the event giving rise to the payment AND such proportions in default of agreement between the Council and the Lessee shall be determined under the provisions of the Arbitration Act 1950 or any statutory modification or re-enactment thereof for the time being in force by a single arbitrator to be appointed by agreement between the Council and the Lessee or in default of agreement by the President for the time being of the Royal Institution of Chartered Surveyors making the appointment at the request of either party.

Faced with this kind of rubbish you might well make the mistake of complaining:

Whilst we understand that the council's legal department may well speak a completely different language to the rest of the country we fail to understand why we should have to stand the expense of getting it translated.

Why indeed? The council that received this complaint thinks it knows the answer:

Referring to the first and penultimate paragraphs of your letter, I can only state that if you feel that you are unable to comprehend the document in its current form, may I suggest or strongly advise that you contact your own independent legal advisor for explanation as to the contents thereto.

As regards to the document being transferred into "Queen's English", without appearing to be difficult, I would inform you that I am at a loss as to what exactly your requirements are.

So that makes two of us.

PLAIN ENGLISH AT WORK

The Plain English Campaign leads the way in effective communication. We specialize in making other people's messages clear and concise.

From internal company correspondence to dealing with the public at large, the Plain English Campaign edits, writes and designs a wide range of material as a professional service. As Chrissie Maher has said, 'Communication has only one purpose – to get information from one person to another. But it fails in an alarmingly high number of cases.'

Here are some choice examples of those 'failures' transformed into 'successes' by the application of the principles of plain English.

From a local authority tenancy agreement:

Before

The Council agrees to be under an obligation to maintain and keep in good repair and working order the installations for space heating, water heating and sanitation including basins, sinks, baths and sanitary conveniences and for the supply of water, gas and electricity but not the fixtures, fittings and appliances for making use of the supply of water, gas and electricity.

After

We will maintain the equipment and fittings for:

- room heating and water heating;
- sanitation (including basins, sinks, baths and toilets); and
- supplying water, gas and electricity.

We will not maintain any other appliances or fittings which use water, gas or electricity.

From a government department:

Before

Consequently, the FAC accepted that controls on saccharin might allow for the acceptable daily intake to be exceeded occasionally by a small number of the population with the most extreme or transitory dietary behaviour. The Committee proposed that the 97.5th percentile could therefore be taken to represent the upper limit of the range of normal consumption in this case.

After

So the Food Advisory Council accepted that a small number of people (about 2.5 per cent of the population) could occasionally take more than the recommended daily amount of saccharin if their diets required it.

The committee said that 97.5 per cent of people take a normal amount of saccharin.

From a London borough leaflet on people's right to vote:

Before

It is important that you shall read the notes, advice and information detailed opposite then complete the form overleaf (all sections) prior to its immediate return to the Council by way of the envelope provided.

After

Please read the notes opposite before you fill in the form. Then send it back to us as soon as possible in the envelope provided.

From an insurance policy:

Before

The due observance and fulfillment of the terms so far as they relate to anything to be done or complied with by the Insured and the truth of the statements and answers in the Proposal shall be conditions precedent to any liability of the Company to make any payment under this Policy.

After

We will only make a payment under this policy if:

- you have kept to the terms of the policy; and
- the statements and answers in your Proposal are true.

A customer's letter to a bus company:

Dear Sir or Madam

This winter my children have been getting cold and wet waiting for the bus home outside the main gate of Devonshire Primary School. I think it is high time you got around to putting up a shelter at the bus stop there.

I have spoken to my local councillor about it. She says you are expecting to get more money soon and I think this shelter should be a priority. I've seen shelters put up in other parts of the town so I'm wondering what you take into account when deciding which ones to build.

If you come out and look at the number of children using the bus stop I am sure you will agree a shelter is needed badly.

Yours faithfully

The bus company's reply:

Dear Madam

With reference to your recent letter in which you submit a request for the provision of a bus passenger shelter in Devon Lane at the bus stop near the main gate of Devonshire Primary School. The stated requirement for a shelter at this location has now been noted, but as you may be aware shelter erection at all locations within our area has been constrained in recent times as a result of reductions in our budgetary allocations from the district councils, and our shelter budget for this Financial Year has already been allocated. Although it seems likely that our budget for shelter provision will be enhanced in the forthcoming Financial Year, it is axiomatic that those prospective shelter sites which have been on our waiting list for long periods of time will be viewed more favourably. However, the attractiveness of sites to potential advertisers and the passenger usage at the sites are also considered by Railroad to be relevant factors in determining whether a shelter can be erected.

Railroad is sympathetic to the claim which you advance, having regard to the changed pattern of bus services in the area, and I would like to offer you the assurance that, consistent with the availability of the necessary resource and subject to an investigation of the site's suitability which will take place in the near future, this location will be considered for inclusion in the shelter programme for the forthcoming Financial Year. It will be appreciated that the site which concerns you cannot be actively considered until the authorisation of the Budget for next year is given in mid-April but you may wish to contact me again at that time to ascertain the latest position vis-a-vis the site that concerns you.

Yours faithfully

Transport Manager

Plain English version of the bus company's reply:

Dear

Thank you for your letter of 1 December asking for a shelter near Devonshire Primary School.

I sympathize with your reasons but unfortunately we have already decided how to use our money for shelters this year. And as you may know, the district councils have given us less money for shelters in recent years.

However, we will look at the site to see if it is suitable for a shelter. If it is, I will add the site to the list of shelters that we will consider in the next financial year starting in April. How many of these we can build will depend on how much money we receive from the district councils. As you say, we expect to get more money for shelters than we did last year.

When we decide which shelters to put up, we consider such things as:

- how long a site has been on the waiting list;
- how many passengers use the stop; and
- how attractive the site is to advertisers.

Perhaps you could contact me again at the end of April. By then we should know whether we can put up a shelter at this site.

Yours sincerely

Before

In order to control book distribution and revisions, publishers and editors shall agree lists of people within the company who have a responsible involvement in individual books or in series of books. Copies shall be stamped and numbered using the stamp design shown in attachment 5 and shall be distributed using a book circulation form according to the document control lists. New editions, amendments and notices of withdrawals shall be sent, also with a book transmittal form to the same recipients. Unstamped copies may be distributed as required, but will not be controlled for updating purposes. Any further circulation of books by recipients should be controlled in a similar manner.

After

To control how books are distributed and revised, publishers and editors must agree a list of people who should be involved with individual books or series of books. The publishers will send these people copies of the books which are stamped and numbered using the stamp design shown in attachment 5. A 'book circulation form' should be sent with each copy. The publisher will also send these people new editions of the books, changes to them, and a notice if the book is withdrawn. Again a 'book circulation form' must be sent to each person. Unstamped copies can be sent out if necessary, but comments on these cannot be taken into account.

Before

The loan is to be used for building works on the borrower's property referred to paragraph 8 below and the loan may not be drawn, in part or in whole, until production to the Bank of an invoice for a sum not less than the amount of the loan in respect of the relevant building works.

After

You must use the loan for the building work on your property named in paragraph 8. You are not allowed to use the loan until we have seen the invoice for the cost of the building work. The invoice must be for at least the same amount as the loan for the building work.

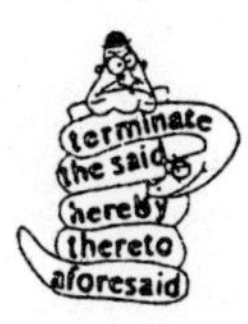

Before

An important aspect of improving quality has been the introduction of medical, dental and multi disciplinary clinical audit as a means of examining current clinical practice and identifying ways of measuring improvements in care and in the outcome of treatment for patients, for example Nursing Indicative Quality Audit and Occupational Therapy and Physiotherapy Audit give professionals the chance to judge their performance against agreed standards.

After

To improve the quality of our services, we have introduced checks (or audits) in all our departments. This means we can look at how we do things, how we can improve and how successful our treatments are. For example, we have audits for our nurses, occupational therapists and physiotherapists so that we, and they, can judge their work against agreed standards.

Utter Drivel!

Before

I understand that a tenancy of any house or flat is granted on the basis of information given in this form. I further understand that if I have knowingly or recklessly given any information which is false or misleading or if I have knowingly or recklessly failed to disclose any information, the Housing Department may be entitled to recover possession of the house or flat under the Housing Act 1980. I undertake to notify the Housing Department of any change in my circumstances.

After

I understand that the council will decide whether to give me a tenancy on the basis of the information on this form. The information I have given is true and complete to the best of my knowledge. I will tell the Housing Department if my circumstances change. I understand that the Housing Department can end my tenancy if I have given any false information through carelessness or deliberate dishonesty.

Before

Your enquiry about the use of the entrance area at the library for the purpose of displaying posters and leaflets about Welfare and Supplementary Benefit rights, gives rise to the question of the provenance and authoritativeness of the material to be displayed.

Posters and leaflets issued by the Central Office of Information, the Department of Health and Social Security and other authoritative bodies are usually displayed in libraries, but items of a disputatious or polemic kind, whilst not necessarily excluded, are considered individually.

After

Thank you for your letter asking permission to put up posters in the entrance area of the library.

Before we can give you an answer we will need to see a copy of the posters to make sure they won't offend anyone.

Before

In the event of any failure or malfunctioning of any component of the apparatus which renders the appliance inoperative and necessitates repair before the appliance will work normally, the company will, at the request of the customer within a reasonable period and during normal working hours repair or replace such components free of charge.

After

If the appliance breaks down because of a faulty part, please tell us. We will then replace or repair the part free of charge within a reasonable time and during our normal working hours.

THE PLAIN ENGLISH A-Z GUIDE TO ALTERNATIVE WORDS

One of the first steps towards clearer writing is to take a critical look at the words and phrases we use.

What follows gives hundreds of plain English alternatives to the pompous and unclear words and phrases that litter official writing. On its own, the guide won't teach you how to write plain English. There's more to it than just replacing 'hard' words with 'easy' ones. But it should help you if you want to get rid of words like 'notwithstanding' and 'expeditiously', and phrases like 'in the majority of instances' and 'at this moment in time'.

If you find yourself about to write, type or dictate a word you wouldn't use in everyday conversation, look it up in the A–Z. You should find a simpler alternative. Often there will be a choice of several words. You need to pick the one that fits best what you are trying to say. Many of these alternatives won't work in every situation or will only work if you re-write your sentence.

A

(an) absence of	no, none
abundance	enough, plenty, a lot (or say how many)
accede to	allow, agree
accelerate	speed up
accentuate	stress
accommodation	where you live, home
accompanying	with
accomplish	do, finish
according to our records	our records show
accordingly	in line with this, so
acknowledge	thank you for
acquaint yourself with	find out about, read
acquiesce	agree
acquire	buy, get
additional	extra, more
adjacent	next to
adjustment	change, alteration
admissible	allowed, acceptable
advantageous	useful, helpful
advise	tell, say (unless you *are* giving advice)
affix	add, write, fasten, stick on, fix to
afford an opportunity	let, allow
afforded	given
aforesaid	this, earlier in this document
aggregate	total
aligned	lined up, in line
alleviate	ease, reduce
allocate	divide, share, add, give
along the lines of	like, as in
alternative	choice, other
alternatively	or, on the other hand
ameliorate	improve, help
amendment	change
anticipate	expect
apparent	clear, plain, obvious, seeming
applicant (the)	you

application	use
appreciable	large, great
apprise	inform, tell
appropriate	proper, right, suitable
appropriate to	suitable for
approximate	about, roughly
as a consequence of	because
as of the date of	from
as regards	about, on the subject of
ascertain	find out
assemble	build, gather, put together
assistance	help
at an early date	soon (or say when)
at its discretion	can, may
at the moment	now (or edit out)
at the present time	now (or edit out)
attempt	try
attend	come to, go to, be at
attributable to	due to, because of
authorize	allow, let
authority	right, power, may
axiomatic	obvious, goes without saying

B

belated	late
beneficial	helpful, useful
bestow	give, award
by means of	by

C

calculate	work out, decide
cease	finish, stop, end

circumvent	get round, avoid, skirt, circle
clarification	explanation, help
combine	mix
combined	together
commence	start, begin
communicate	talk, write, telephone (be specific)
competent	able, can
compile	make, collect
complete	fill in, finish
completion	end
comply with	keep to, meet
component	is made up of, includes
(it is) compulsory	(you) must
conceal	hide
concerning	about, on
conclusion	end
concur	agree
condition	rule
consequently	so
considerable	great, important
constitutes	makes up, forms, is
construe	interpret
consult	talk to, meet, ask
consumption	amount used
contemplate	think about
contrary to	against, despite, different
correct	put right
correspond	write
costs the sum of	costs
counter	against
courteous	polite
cumulative	add up, added up
currently	now (or edit out)
customary	usual, normal

D

deduct	take off, take away
deem to be	treat as
defer	put off, delay
deficiency	lack of
delete	cross out
demonstrate	show, prove
denote	show
depict	show
designate	point out, show, name
desire	wish, want
despatch or dispatch	send, post
despite the fact that	though, although
determine	decide, work out, set, end
detrimental	harmful, damaging
difficulties	problems
diminish	lessen, reduce
disburse	pay, pay out
discharge	carry out
disclose	tell, show
disconnect	cut off, unplug
discontinue	stop, end
discrete	separate
discuss	talk about
disseminate	spread
documentation	papers, documents
domiciled in	living in
dominant	main
due to the fact that	because, as
duration	time, life
during which time	while
dwelling	home

E

economical	cheap, good value
eligible	allowed, qualified
elucidate	explain, make clear
emphasize	stress
empower	allow, let
enable	allow
enclosed	inside, with
(please find) enclosed	I enclose
encounter	meet
endeavour	try
enquire	ask
ensure	make sure
envisage	expect, imagine
equivalent	equal, the same
erroneous	wrong
establish	show, find out, set up
evaluate	test, check
evince	show, prove
ex officio	because of his or her position
exceptionally	only when, in this case
excessive	too many, too much
exclude	leave out
excluding	apart from, except
exclusively	only
exempt from	free from
expedite	hurry, speed up
expeditiously	as soon as possible, quickly
expenditure	spending
expire	run out
extant	current, in force
extremity	limit

F

fabricate	make, make up
facilitate	help, make possible
factor	reason
failure to	if you do not
finalize	end, finish
following	after
for the duration of	during, while
for the purpose of	to, for
for the reason that	because
formulate	plan, devise
forthwith	now, at once
forward	send
frequently	often
furnish	give
further to	after, following
furthermore	then, also, and

G

generate	produce, give, make
give consideration to	consider, think about
grant	give

H

henceforth	from now on, from today
hereby	now, by this (or edit out)
herein	here (or edit out)
hereinafter	after this (or edit out)
hereof	of this
hereto	to this

heretofore	until now, previously
hereunder	below
herewith	with this (or edit out)
hitherto	until now
hold in abeyance	wait, postpone
hope and trust	hope, trust (but not both)

I

if and when	if, when (but not both)
illustrate	show, explain
immediately	at once, now
implement	carry out, do
imply	suggest, hint at
in a number of cases	some (or say how many)
in accordance with	as, under, because of
in addition to	and, as well as, also
in advance	before
in case of	if
in conjunction with	and, with
in connection with	for, about
in consequence	because, as
in excess of	more than
in lieu of	instead of
in order that	to
in receipt of	get, have, receive
in relation to	about
in respect of	about, for
in the absence of	without
in the case of	in, for
in the course of	while, during
in the event of/that	if
in the majority of instances	most, mostly
in the near future	soon
in the neighbourhood of	about, around

in view of the fact that	as, because
inappropriate	wrong, unsuitable
inception	start, beginning
incorporating	which includes
incurred	have to pay, owe
indicate	show, suggest
inform	tell
initially	at first
initiate	begin, start
insert	put in
inspect	look at
instances	cases
intend to	will
intimate	say, hint
irrespective of	despite, even if
is in accordance with	agrees with, follows
is of the opinion	thinks
issue	give, send
it is known that	I/we know that

J

jeopardize	risk, threaten

L

(a) large number of	many, most (or say how many)
locality	place, area
locate	find, put

M

magnitude	size
(it is) mandatory	(you) must
manner	way
manufacture	make
marginal	small, slight
material	relevant
materialize	happen, occur
may in the future	may, might, could
merchandise	goods
mislay	lose
modification	change
moreover	and, also, as well

N

necessitate	have to, need to, must
negligible	very small
nevertheless	but, however, even so
notify	tell, let us know
notwithstanding	even if, despite, still, yet
numerous	many (or say how many)

O

objective	aim, goal
(it is) obligatory	(you) must
obtain	get, receive
occasioned by	caused by, because of
on behalf of	for
on numerous occasions	often

on receipt	when we (you) get
on request	if you ask
on the grounds that	because
on the occasion that	when, if
operate	work, run
optimum	best, ideal
option	choice
ordinarily	normally, usually
otherwise	or
outstanding	unpaid
owing to	because of

P

partially	partly
participate	join in, take part
particulars	details, facts
per annum	a year
(a) percentage of	some (or say what percentage)
perform	do
permissible	allowed
permit	let, allow
personnel	people, staff
persons	people, anyone
peruse	read, read carefully, look at
place	put
possess	have, own
possessions	belongings
practically	almost, nearly
predominant	main
prescribed	set, fixed
preserve	keep, protect
previous	earlier, before, last
principal	main
prior to	before
proceed	go ahead

procure	get, obtain, arrange
profusion of	plenty, too many (or say how many)
prohibit	ban, stop
projected	estimated
prolonged	long
promptly	quickly, at once
promulgate	advertise
proportion	part
provide	give
provided that	if, as long as
provisions	rules, terms
proximity	close, closeness, near
purchase	buy
pursuant to	under, because of, in line with

Q

qualify for	can, get, be able to get

R

reconsider	think again, look again
reduce	cut
reduction	cut
referred to as	called
refers to	talks about, mentions
(have) regard to	take into account
regarding	about, on
regulation	rule
reimburse	repay, pay back
reiterate	repeat, restate
relating to	about
remain	stay

remainder	the rest, what is left
remittance	payment
remuneration	pay, wages, salary
render	make, give, send
report	tell
represents	shows, stands for, is
request	ask, question
require	need, want, force
requirements	needs, rules
reside	live
residence	home, where you live
restriction	limit
retain	keep
reverse	back
review	look at (again)
revised	new, changed

S

said/such/same	the, this, that
scrutinize	read (look at) carefully
select	choose
settle	pay
similarly	also, in the same way
solely	only
specified	given, written, set
state	say, tell us, write down
statutory	legal, by law
subject to	depending on, under, keeping to
submit	send, give
subsequent to/upon	after
subsequently	later
substantial	large, great, a lot of
substantially	more or less
sufficient	enough

supplement	go with, add to
supplementary	extra, more
supply	give, sell, deliver

T

(the) tenant	you
terminate	stop, end
that being the case	if so
the question as to whether	whether
thereafter	then, afterwards
thereby	by that, because of that
therein	in that, there
thereto	to that
thus	so, therefore
to date	so far, up to now
to the extent that	if, when
transfer	change, move
transmit	send

U

ultimately	in the end, finally
unavailability	lack of
undernoted	the following
undersigned	I, we
undertake	agree, promise, do
uniform	same, similar
unilateral	one-sided, one way
unoccupied	empty
until such time	until
utilization	use
utilize	use

V

variation	change
virtually	almost (or edit out)
visualize	see, predict

W

ways and means	ways
we have pleasure in	we are glad to
whatsoever	whatever, what, any
whensoever	when
whereas	but
whether or not	whether
with a view to	to
with effect from	from
with reference to	about
with regard to	about, for
with respect to	about, for
with the minimum of delay	quickly (or say when)

Y

you are requested to	please
your attention is drawn	please see, please note

Z

zero-rate	free, free of
zone	area, region

Words and phrases to avoid

The words and phrases below often crop up in letters and reports. Often you can remove them from a sentence without changing the meaning or the tone. In other words, they add nothing to the message. Try leaving them out of your writing. You'll find your sentences survive and succeed without them.

- a total of
- absolutely
- abundantly
- actually
- all things being equal
- as a matter of fact
- as far as I am concerned
- at the end of the day
- at this moment in time
- basically
- current
- currently
- during the period from
- each and every one
- existing
- extremely
- I am of the opinion that
- I would like to say
- I would like to take this opportunity to
- in due course
- in other words
- in the end
- in the final analysis
- in this connection
- in total
- in view of the fact that
- it should be understood
- last but not least
- obviously
- of course
- other things being equal
- quite
- really
- really quite
- regarding the (noun), it was
- the fact of the matter is
- the month(s) of
- to all intents and purposes
- to one's own mind
- very